HarperCollins Sir

SENTENCE
WRITING
SIMPLIFIED

Norwood Selby

Surry Community College

HarperCollinsCollegePublishers

Cover ...

Production ... **tor:** Paula Keller

Compositor: Graphic Sciences Corporation

Printer and Binder: R. R. Donnelley & Sons Company

Cover Printer: The Lehigh Press, Inc.

Sentence Writing Simplified

Copyright © 1992 by T. Norwood Selby

ISBN 0-06-501149-X

94 95 9 8 7 6 5 4 3 2

Contents

PUNCTUATION AND MECHANICS

Preface

Sentence Writing Simplified is a brief yet thorough grammar and punctuation guide for students of composition, office personnel who need an easy-to-use desk reference, or anyone else who wants to ensure that his or her written communications are clear and correct.

Part I presents the basics of grammar—the parts of speech, phrases, and clauses—in a logical way. Definitions and explanations are repeated when necessary; readers who don't go through the text from front to back will not be lost. Four chapters, Chapters 5 through 8, show how to construct sentences that are not only grammatically correct but also are interesting and varied.

In Part II, punctuation is explained in clear-cut rules, offering a concise yet complete guide to all of the major punctuation rules of Standard English. Each of the most confusing marks of punctuation is covered in a separate chapter.

Clear explanations, numerous examples, and a comprehensive index make *Sentence Writing Simplified* an ideal reference to grammar and punctuation.

Norwood Selby

SENTENCE WRITING SIMPLIFIED

GRAMMAR

1

Verbs, Subjects, and Complements

In this book we break the study of language down into basic steps. Study each step until you feel you understand it before moving on to the next.

Subjects and Predicates

A normal English sentence contains both a **subject** and a **predicate**. **A subject is what is talked about in a sentence**.

John drives a 1966 Mustang.
> *John* is the subject of the sentence. He is being talked about in the sentence.

A predicate says something about the subject. In the sentence above, *drives a 1966 Mustang* is the predicate. It says something about John.

A sentence can be composed of just a subject and a predicate.

Mary sews.
> *Mary* is the subject. She is being talked about in the sentence. *Sews* is the predicate. The word *sews* says something about Mary.

More often, however, a sentence contains more than just a subject and predicate.

A tall man with red hair walked into a restaurant.
> The subject of the sentence is *man*. He is being talked about. *Walked* is the predicate in the sentence. It says something about the man (subject).

The sentence is said to have a **complete subject** and a **complete predicate**. The complete subject contains the basic subject *man* (called the **simple subject**) and all the words that relate to the subject. Thus, the complete subject is *A tall man with red hair. A, tall*, and *with red hair* all relate to *man*. The complete predicate contains the predicate itself *walked* (called a **simple predicate**) and all the words that relate to it. Thus, *walked into a restaurant* is the complete predicate. *Into a restaurant* relates to *walked*.

> The tired student stretched out for a nap.
> The complete subject is *The tired student.*
> The complete predicate is *stretched out for a nap.*

The key word in the complete predicate is the verb. *Stretched* is the verb in the sentence above because it is the key word that says something about the subject.

Recognizing Verbs

Action Verbs

Verbs are often the most important words in sentences. When you can recognize them, you are on your way. Everything else in a sentence relates to the verb either directly or indirectly. The easiest verbs to recognize are those which show action. Words such as *run, jump, play, sing*, and *drive* can clearly show action.

> The boxer <u>jumps</u> rope for fifteen minutes every day.
> *Jumps* is the verb.

Not all action verbs show physical action. Many verbs in English express mental action; these include *think, believe, imagine*, and *wonder.* They are also action verbs; they just express a different kind of action. As you know, thinking can be hard work; it is an active process.

> The executives <u>think</u> about the company's problems every morning.
> *Think* is an action verb.

Linking Verbs

Some verbs do not show action. Instead they link the subject to another word, phrase, or clause that names or describes it. Thus they are known as linking verbs. The various forms of the verb *be* are the most common linking verbs. The verb *be* is very irregular and takes many forms (for example, *is, was, are, am, were, being,* and *been*). By examining a few examples, you will see how forms of the verb *be* link parts of sentences together.

> Jane is tall.
> > *Is* is a linking verb.

The word *is* does not show action. Instead, *is* establishes a connection, or equivalency, between *Jane* and *tall*. It links the woman to an attribute describing her, and so it is known as a linking verb.

> I am a student.
> > *Am* is a linking verb.

Notice that the verb *am* links the word *I* to the word *student*. It is a linking verb.

Though forms of *be* are the most common linking verbs, they are not the only ones. Many verbs that refer to the senses are linking verbs.

Words such as *feel, taste, sound, smell,* and *look* can be linking verbs, though they do not always have to be (see the section on correct usage of adjectives and adverbs, Chapter 10). Other linking verbs are *become, seem,* and *appear*. Here are some linking verbs:

is		feel
am		taste
was	any form	sound
were	of the	smell
been	verb *be*	look
being		become
		seem
		appear

> The pie tastes sour.
> > *Tastes* links *pie* to *sour*.

The girl <u>became</u> a champion fiddler.
Became links *girl* to *fiddler*.

Auxiliary Verbs

An auxiliary verb precedes the main verb and helps it do its job. The auxiliary verb may make the main verb more precise in describing and telling when things happen. It may indicate obligation, possibility, emphasis, or permission.

> The man <u>will complete</u> the project.
>> The main verb is *complete*, and the auxiliary verb is *will*. The auxiliary verb tells you that the action has not yet been completed. It will be completed, however, sometime in the future.

> Ralph <u>has ended</u> his five-year probation.
>> The main verb is *ended*, and the auxiliary is *has*. The auxiliary verb tells you that the action has been completed.

> You <u>must complete</u> the assignment.
>> The main verb is *complete*; the auxiliary is *must*. The auxiliary indicates that the act of completing is an obligation.

> I <u>do know</u> the answer to that question.
>> The main verb is *know*; the auxiliary is *do*. The auxiliary emphasizes the act of knowing.

Some common auxiliary verbs are *may, might, must, do, did, could, should, is, am, are, was, were, has, had, have,* and *will.* Sometimes only one of these auxiliaries will be used with the main verb. Sometimes more than one will be used.

> You <u>are working</u> behind the counter this afternoon.
> Evelyn Smith <u>will be working</u> behind the counter next week.
> John Coppleton <u>is being assigned</u> behind the counter next week.

In each of the examples the last word in the word group (*working* and *assigned*) is the main verb. The other words underlined as part of the verb are auxiliaries. The auxiliaries formed from *be* help to identify the time of the action.

Note: Forms of *be* can be auxiliaries of other verbs. A form of *be* is a linking verb if it is the main verb in the sentence. Example: This sentence is short. *Is* is a linking verb that links the word *sentence* to the word *short*. There is no other verb in the sentence, so *is* cannot be an auxiliary verb.

> My professor is teaching me English.
> *Is* is not a linking verb because it is not the main verb in the sentence. It is an auxiliary verb that precedes the main verb *teaching* and tells when the teaching is being done.

Auxiliary verbs do not always occur side by side with main verbs. In fact, when an auxiliary is used to form a question, the auxiliary occurs earlier in the sentence than the main verb.

> Has the man completed the cabinets?
> *Has* is the auxiliary of the main verb *completed*.

Sometimes the auxiliaries themselves are separated:

> Is the movie being filmed today?
> *Is* and *being* are auxiliaries of the main verb *filmed*.

When auxiliaries are used to introduce questions, the easiest way to analyze the sentence is by turning the question into a statement:

> **Question:** Has the man completed the cabinets?
> **Statement:** The man *has completed* the cabinets. (Auxiliary and main verb are now together.)

Recognizing Subjects

The second step in learning the basics of English grammar is to be able to recognize the subject. After you have found the verb, you should then find the subject. You find it by asking Who or What? in front of the verb.

> John swept the sidewalk.
> Who or what swept? **John**

Jane considered the problem for three hours.
Who or what considered? **Jane**

The computer saved the company a fortune.
Who or what saved the company a fortune? **computer**

Obviously, **the subject is a naming word**. The subject of an action verb names the doer of the action. In the sample sentences just presented, John does the action of sweeping, Jane does the action of considering, and the computer does the action of saving.

Like any other subject, the subject of a linking verb is a naming word. Also like any other subject, the subject of a linking verb can be found by asking Who or What? in front of the verb.

Gene Caudill is president of the Exeter Company.
Who or what is? **Gene Caudill**

The machine is a constant source of trouble.
Who or what is? **machine**

The sample sentences above follow the most common order an English sentence takes: subject-verb. However, not all sentences in English follow the subject-verb order. Sentences beginning with the word *there* usually alter the subject-verb order. Don't mistake the expletive *there* for the subject. It merely indicates that the subject will follow the verb. (An expletive like *there* only serves as a filler and does not contribute to the meaning of the sentence.)

subject
There are four girls on the Little League team.

If you get in the habit of finding the verb and then asking Who or What? in front of it, you should have no trouble with sentences that are not in the subject-verb order. In the preceding example sentence, if you know that *are* is the verb and ask Who or What are? you will easily see that the subject is *girls*.

subject
Is Robert making a new piece for the machine?

The sentence is not in the subject-verb order. It is in the auxiliary-subject-verb order. If you ask Who or What is making? you will see that the answer is *Robert*, the subject. The easiest way to find the subject and verb in such a sentence is to turn the question *Is Robert making a new piece for the machine?* into a statement: *Robert is making a new piece for the machine.* Now the sentence is in the subject-verb order.

Recognizing Compound Subjects and Compound Verbs

The next step in being able to recognize subjects and verbs is realizing that they may be compounded; that is, two or more subjects or two or more verbs may be joined together by the words *and, or, nor, but.*

> John, Bob, and Ralph went to the game together.
>> The compound subjects are *John, Bob,* and *Ralph.*

> Tony Arrowsmith sings well but dances clumsily.
>> The compound verbs are *sings* and *dances.*

> Jane said she would either trade the car or sell it.
>> The compound verbs are *trade* or *sell.*

To find a compound subject, you must find the verb first and ask Who or What? in front of it.

> Bob Smith, Elaine Frank, and John Bartlett are competent engineers.
>> Who or what are? The compound subject is *Bob Smith, Elaine Frank,* and *John Bartlett.*

> Television, radios, newspapers, and magazines help to keep people well informed.
>> Who or what keep? The compound subject is *television, radios, newspapers,* and *magazines.*

In some sentences, both subjects and verbs are compound.

> Joan Burger and Tony Arrowsmith sing and dance well together.

The compound subject is *Joan Burger* and *Tony Arrowsmith,* and the compound verb is *sing* and *dance.* Of course, sentences with compound subjects and compound verbs can vary from the subject-verb order like any other sentences.

> There are three men and four women on the committee.
>> The compound subject is *men* and *women*. The verb is *are*.

> Are Ed Shoenbaum and Lorraine Chute entering or leaving?
>> *Ed Shoenbaum* and *Lorraine Chute* is the subject, and *are entering* and *leaving* is the verb.

Recognizing Complements

Once you can recognize subjects and verbs, you can move on to the next step in sentence analysis, recognizing complements. A complement is a word that completes the meaning of the subject and the predicate. The four most important complements are (1) **direct objects**, (2) **indirect objects**, (3) **predicate nominatives**, and (4) **predicate adjectives**.

Direct Objects

Not all verbs take direct objects. The direct object receives the action of the verb, and so the verb must express action before there can be a receiver of the action. When a verb has a direct object, the object generally appears in a sentence after the subject and verb. Remember: you find the verb first; then you find the subject. Just as you asked Who or What? *before* the verb to find the subject, you ask Whom or What? *after* the verb to find the direct object.

> Mary made a mistake.
>> Clearly, *made* is the verb in the sentence. Now ask Who or what? in front of the verb: Who or what made? Mary. *Mary* is the subject. To find the direct object, ask whom or what after the verb: Mary made whom or what? mistake. *Mistake* is the direct object.

The following chart indicates which questions to ask, where to ask them, and which order to ask them in.

Mary made a mistake.

<pre>
        2   1   3
  Subject (Who? ← Verb →   (Whom? → Direct Object
         What?)   What?)
       ↓   ↓   ↓
     Mary   made   mistake
</pre>

Be very careful to ask your questions before the verb when looking for the subject and after the verb when looking for the direct object. Since both subjects and direct objects are naming words, a direct object will answer a subject's question and vice versa. Therefore, if you ask the right question in the wrong place, you will get the wrong answer.

In looking for direct objects you must consider other things besides the questions they answer, however. One of the main points to keep in mind is that not *all* sentences have direct objects. Note the following example:

John swims every day.
    John is the subject and *swims* is the verb.
    There is no direct object.

Clearly, not all action verbs take direct objects.

Remember, too, that only action verbs can take direct objects. Note the following example:

The animal is a deer.
    There cannot be a direct object since the verb is the linking verb *is* and not an action verb.

On the other hand:

This company produces ten cars an hour.
    The verb *produces* is an action verb; it can and does take a direct object—*cars*.

It is easy to remember that only action verbs can take direct objects when you understand what direct objects are. Direct objects receive the action of the verb. There must be action before there can be a receiver of the action.

In the sentence *The company produces ten cars an hour*, the cars receive the action of being produced. In the sentence *John loves Beth Henson very much*, Beth Henson receives the action of being loved. In both of these sentences the receiver of the action is the direct object. The direct objects answer the question Whom or What? asked after the verb:

The company produces <u>what</u>?
        Cars is the direct object.

John loves <u>whom</u>?
        Beth Henson is the direct object.

Notice that the most common pattern for sentences containing direct objects is subject-verb-object.

        s.   v.   d.o.
The company produces ten cars an hour.

    s.   v.   d.o.
John loves Beth Henson very much.

Though the most common pattern for sentences containing direct objects is subject-verb-object, do not assume that is the only pattern.

Does John play golf often?
        Notice *does* is an auxiliary, *John* is the subject, *play* is the main verb, and *golf* is the direct object. The pattern is auxiliary-subject-verb-object.

    aux.   s.   v.   d.o.
Do computers solve problems quickly?

Like verbs and subjects, direct objects can also be compound.

            d.o.   d.o.   d.o.
John loves golf, tennis, and skiing.

A Checklist for Direct Objects
A direct object must:

1.   Be a naming word.
2.   Be in the predicate.
3.   Follow an action verb.
4.   Answer the questions: "What?" or "Whom?"

Indirect Objects

After learning to recognize subjects, verbs, and direct objects, the next sentence part you need to look for is the indirect object. Like subjects and direct objects, indirect objects are naming words. You can find an indirect object if it is present by asking To or for whom? or To or for what? after the direct object.

        s.   v.   d.o.
    Bruce gave Martha a ring.
        Bruce gave a ring to or for whom? *Martha* is the indirect object.

            s.   v.   d.o.
    The philanthropist gave the museum a million dollars.
        The philanthropist gave dollars to or for what? *Museum* is the indirect object.

Remember: The indirect object is the fourth sentence element you try to find. Be sure you ask the right question in the right place.

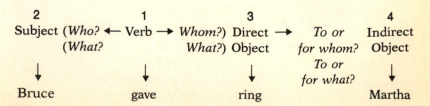

Most sentences will not contain indirect objects, because only a few verbs can take them. Here are examples of some of the verbs that can take indirect objects: *give, bring, buy, present, throw,* and *award.*

Even though the indirect object is the fourth sentence part you try to find, it is generally located in the sentence before the direct object. The most natural order is subject-verb-indirect object-direct object. Note the following examples:

s.	v.	i.o.	d.o.

The quarterback threw his receiver a perfect pass.

s.	v.	i.o.	d.o.

The committee awarded Sara the prize.

Of course, when the sentence is a question, the order may change.

aux.	s.	v.	i.o.	d.o.

Did the executive buy her office a new typewriter?

But such a sentence fits the pattern of subject-verb-indirect object-direct object if you turn it around into a statement.

s.	v.	i.o.	d.o.

The executive did buy her office a new typewriter.

One thing to remember when studying indirect objects is that you must mentally supply the words *to* or *for* before the *whom* or *what.* If the sentence has the *to* or *for* expressed, the word cannot be an indirect object.

The quarterback threw a perfect pass (to) his receiver.

Since the *to* is expressed, the word *receiver* cannot be an indirect object. Which of the following sentences contains an indirect object?

1. The team presented the coach a new trophy case.
2. The team presented a new trophy case to the coach.
   Sentence 1 contains the indirect object since you mentally supply the missing *to*: The team presented (to) the coach a new trophy case.

A Checklist for Indirect Objects
An indirect object must:

1. Be a naming word.
2. Be in the predicate.
3. Follow an action verb.
4. Answer the question: "To whom?" "To what?" "For whom?" "For what?"

Predicate Nominatives

Only action verbs can take direct and indirect objects. However, linking verbs take complements. One such complement is the predicate nominative. A predicate nominative is a naming word (noun or pronoun) that follows a linking verb and renames the subject.

p.n.
Jane Martinez is a psychologist.
> *Psychologist* is a naming word that follows the linking verb *is* and renames the subject *Jane Martinez. Psychologist* is a predicate nominative.

p.n.
John Smith was an explorer.
> *Explorer* is a naming word that follows the linking verb *was* and renames the subject *John Smith. Explorer* is a predicate nominative.

Since the predicate nominative is linked to the subject by the verb, sentences containing predicate nominatives have linking verbs rather than action verbs.

p.n.
The Eagles are a good team.
> The verb *are* links the predicate nominative *team* to the subject *Eagles*.

Of course, not all linking verbs have predicate nominatives, just as not all action verbs have direct objects.

> John Tybalt is handsome.
>> There is no other word in the sentence that renames the subject *John Tybalt*. Therefore, the sentence does not contain a predicate nominative.

A Checklist for Predicate Nominatives

A predicate nominative must:

1. Be a naming word.
2. Be in the predicate part of the sentence.
3. Follow a linking verb.
4. Mean the same or rename the subject.

Predicate Adjectives

A predicate adjective is a word (adjective) that usually follows a linking verb and qualifies, limits, or describes (modifies) the subject.

> p.a.
> Jane is happy.
>> *Happy* is an adjective that follows the linking verb *is* and modifies the subject *Jane*. *Happy* describes *Jane*. *Happy* is a predicate adjective.

> p.a.
> The computer is expensive.
>> *Expensive* is an adjective that follows the linking verb *is* and modifies the subject *computer*. *Expensive* is a predicate adjective.

A predicate adjective is linked to the word it modifies by a linking verb. Remember: Both predicate adjectives and predicate nominatives are used with linking verbs.

A Checklist for Predicate Adjectives
A predicate adjective must:

1. Be an adjective.
2. Be in the predicate part of the sentence.
3. Follow a linking verb.
4. Modify the subject.

2

Parts of Speech

The part of speech of a word depends on the way the word is used in a particular sentence. Therefore, the same word can be any of several parts of speech. For example:

Blue is my favorite color. (noun)
My father drives a blue truck. (adjective)
Mark is blueing his gun barrel. (verb)

Before you can understand the parts of speech, however, you must be familiar with their definitions. The definitions tell you how the word may be used. If you know the part of speech of every word in a sentence, then you know what every word in that sentence does. There are eight parts of speech: *nouns*, *pronouns*, *adjectives*, *verbs*, *adverbs*, *prepositions*, *conjunctions*, and *interjections*.

Nouns

Nouns are naming words. They name people, places, things, and ideas—*Robert*, *England*, *tire*, and *justice*.

Robert names a person.
England names a place.
Tire names a thing.
Justice names an idea.

Subjects are naming words as well. A noun, however, is merely a way of identifying how a word is used in a sentence. A subject, on the other hand, is a word that tells what is talked about in a sentence. Clearly, most subjects will be nouns. However, there may be many nouns in a sentence that don't tell what is being talked about. For instance,

> Bob lent <u>Mary</u> the <u>key</u> to the <u>car</u>.
> Only the noun <u>Bob</u> is the subject. But the underlined words <u>Mary</u>, <u>key</u>, and <u>car</u> are all nouns.

Some nouns name more specifically than others. *Ms. Smith, woman, lady, person, mother, wife, Jane Everette Smith* are all nouns that might identify the same person. *Ms. Smith* and *Jane Everette Smith* both name more specifically than the other words; they are known as proper nouns. A *proper noun* is capitalized and names a specific person, place, or thing. *Chicago* is a proper noun and so is *Mississippi River. Woman, lady, person, mother*, and *wife* are all common nouns. A *common noun* names a general class of people or things and is not capitalized. Words such as *city* and *river* are common nouns. As you can see, nouns are quite versatile. They can also name things as concrete as *sand* and *wood* and as abstract as *freedom* and *justice.*

Pronouns

Pronouns are naming words that are used to take the place of nouns. *John* is a noun; *he* is a pronoun. *Team* is a noun; *they* is a pronoun. Pronouns name in an even more general manner than common nouns. Subjects, direct objects, and indirect objects are either nouns or pronouns. Pronouns are important in making sentences easier to read. Without them English sentences would be choppy and repetitious.

Since pronouns take the place of nouns, it is not difficult to understand their function. However, many people have trouble identifying pronouns because there are so many kinds. Rather than worrying about all the different kinds, refer to the following list of words commonly used as pronouns:

I	they	anyone	whom
my	them	anybody	whoever
me	their	everyone	whomever
you	we	everybody	myself
your	us	no one	yourself

he	our	none	himself
his	many	each	herself
him	some	this	itself
she	few	that	ourselves
her	both	these	themselves
it	several	those	all
its	one	who	

Adjectives

Adjectives are words that describe, clarify, or limit (modify) a noun or pronoun. They are usually easy to recognize because they answer the questions Which one? What kind? How many? One-word adjectives generally come before the words they modify.

> adj. n.
> big car
> > Which car? big

> adj.   n.
> Siamese cat
> > What kind of cat? Siamese

> adj.   n.
> three men
> > How many men? three

One kind of adjective is extremely easy to identify—the *article*. The articles are *a, an,* and *the.* Remember, however, "article" does not name a part of speech. *A, an,* and *the* are adjectives.

Some adjectives can be confusing. Words such as *his, your, my, her, our, their,* and *its* are as much pronouns as adjectives.

> John keeps *his* car in good shape.

His is a pronoun taking the place of the noun *John.* At the same time, however, *his* is an adjective modifying the subject *car.* Some people call words like these pronominal adjectives; others call them adjectival pronouns. It is not important which part of speech you prefer to call them; the important thing to remember is that they fit the definitions of both pronouns and adjectives at the same time.

Verbs

The first thing you did in Chapter 1 was to recognize verbs. By now you should be able to recognize them easily. However, you should know other things about verbs besides how to recognize them. You should realize that **verbs are either regular or irregular and that they have tense, voice, number, and mood**.

Regular and Irregular Verbs

Look at the following model:

1. I _____ today.

2. I _____ yesterday.

3. I have _____.

4. I am _____-ing.

Fill each blank with the appropriate form of the same verb; the forms are known as the principal parts of the verb. The first principal part is called the *simple present*. The second is the *simple past*. The third principal part is called the *past participle*; notice that the third principal part must be preceded by an auxiliary, such as *have*. The fourth principal part is known as the *present participle* and is also preceded by an auxiliary, such as *am*.

A *regular verb* forms the simple past and past participle by adding *-ed* to the simple present, and it forms the present participle by adding *-ing* to the simple present.

I *play* today.	simple present
I *played* yesterday.	simple past
I have *played*.	past participle
I am *playing*.	present participle

An *irregular verb* usually forms its simple past and past participle by changing a vowel of the simple present. The present participle of an irregular verb is formed in the same manner as a regular verb, by adding *-ing* to the simple present.

I *begin* today.	simple present
I *began* yesterday.	simple past
I have *begun.*	past participle
I am *beginning.*	present participle

If you are not sure you can correctly fill in the blanks of the model with the appropriate form of a verb, refer to the following partial list of irregular verbs or, preferably, to a dictionary.

Simple Present	Simple Past	Aux. + Past Participle	Aux. + Present Participle
am	was	been	being
begin	began	begun	beginning
bite	bit	bitten	biting
blow	blew	blown	blowing
break	broke	broken	breaking
bring	brought	brought	bringing
burst	burst	burst	bursting
choose	chose	chosen	choosing
come	came	come	coming
draw	drew	drawn	drawing
drink	drank	drunk	drinking
drive	drove	driven	driving
eat	ate	eaten	eating
fall	fell	fallen	falling
forsake	forsook	forsaken	forsaking
hear	heard	heard	hearing
lay	laid	laid	laying
lead	led	led	leading
lie	lay	lain	lying
ring	rang	rung	ringing
rise	rose	risen	rising
see	saw	seen	seeing
set	set	set	setting

show	showed	shown	showing
sit	sat	sat	sitting
slay	slew	slain	slaying
steal	stole	stolen	stealing
throw	threw	thrown	throwing
wake	woke (waked)	waked	waking
wear	wore	worn	wearing
write	wrote	written	writing

A common error in using principal parts is failing to put the final -*d* on a word. Though the final -*d* may not always be noticed in speech, its absence in writing is readily apparent.

Incorrect: I use to be a good speller.
Correct: I used to be a good speller.
Incorrect: I was suppose to finish my lab report.
Correct: I was supposed to finish my lab report.

Also, do not use the past participle as though it were the simple past: *I done the job* and *I seen that movie.* Instead, use the proper form of the verb:

I did the job.
I saw that movie.

Tense

The tense of a verb indicates time. There are only six basic tenses: present, past, future, present perfect, past perfect, and future perfect.

The *present tense* indicates an action that is going on at the present time or that occurs habitually.

The man <u>looks</u> off into the distance.
Looks reflects an action going on at the present time.

The seasons <u>change</u> four times a year.
Change reflects an action that occurs habitually.

Sometimes the present tense indicates future action.

My plane <u>leaves</u> at 5:00 P.M.
Leaves indicates an action that will occur in the future.

The present tense is also used to express general truths.

Water <u>freezes</u> at 32 degrees Fahrenheit.

The *past tense* indicates an action completed at a specific time in the past.

Luis Astorga <u>broke</u> his arm last week.
Broke indicates a completed past action.

The *future tense* indicates an action that will take place in the future.

Ms. Jones <u>will repair</u> the television set tomorrow.
Will repair indicates an action to be performed in the future.

The "perfect" tenses always contain a form of the verb *have (have, has, had)* and the past participle.

The *present perfect tense* is formed from the appropriate present tense form of the verb *have (has* or *have)* plus the past participle and indicates an action that is completed at the present time or that is continuing into the present.

Norman Mailer <u>has completed</u> the research for his new book.
Has completed indicates an action completed at the present time.

I <u>have played</u> golf for many years.
Have played indicates an action continuing into the present.

The *past perfect tense* is formed from the past tense form of the verb *have (had)* plus the past participle and indicates an action completed before a specific time in the past.

The girl <u>had broken</u> the vase before her mother could get there.
Had broken indicates an action completed before the mother's arrival.

The *future perfect tense* is formed from the future tense of the verb *have (will have* or *shall have)* plus the past participle and indicates an action that will be completed before a specific time in the future.

The teacher <u>will have graded</u> the papers before class tomorrow.
> *Will have graded* indicates an action that will be completed before class time tomorrow.

Some writers unnecessarily shift from one tense to another. For example, in the sentence *During the meeting Mr. Oliver explained the need for a tax increase while Mr. Leer explains the disadvantages*, there is no reason to shift from the past tense used for Mr. Oliver to the present tense used for Mr. Leer. Such shifts can greatly confuse readers.

Voice

Each verb tense can be either in the *active voice* or the *passive voice*. In the active voice the subject is the doer of the action. In the passive voice the subject is the receiver of the action. The passive voice is composed of a form of the auxiliary verb *be (am, are, is, was, were)* followed by a past participle.

Nelson played the game.
> The verb *played* is in the active voice because the subject *Nelson* is doing the action.
> Who or what played? Nelson

The game was played by Nelson.
> The verb *was played* is in the passive voice because the subject *game* is the receiver of the action.
> Who or what was played? Game

The passive voice is formed from the active voice first by making the direct object of the active sentence become the subject of the passive sentence:

Original Sentence: Nelson played the game. → The game . . .

Next, by inserting the form of the auxiliary *be* that is the same tense as the original sentence followed by the past participle of the original active verb:

Nelson played the game. → The game was played . . .

Finally, by making the original subject of the active sentence come after the past participle and after a word such as *by* in the passive sentence:

> **Active:** Nelson played the game. →
> **Passive:** The game was played by Nelson.

Though good writers consider the active voice to be stronger and therefore better than the passive voice, you need to know both. Because the passive voice deemphasizes the doer of the action, it is often used to soften the effect of a complaint. In speaking to the letter carrier, you are much more polite when you say *My magazine was torn* than when you say *You tore my magazine*. Also, there are times when the doer of the action is unknown, as in the sentence *The letter was not signed*. Nevertheless, try to keep your writing in the active voice. The active voice is much more direct since the subject clearly performs the action.

Be sure to avoid needless shifts from active voice to passive voice and vice versa.

> John <u>played</u> football for three years in high school, but the sport <u>was</u> not <u>enjoyed</u> by him.
> > There is a needless shift from the active voice to the passive voice. Rewrite the sentence to say: John *played* football for three years in high school, but he *did* not *enjoy* the sport.

Person and Number

The *number* of a verb simply indicates whether the verb is singular or plural.

> The boy <u>sings</u>. (singular)
> The boys <u>sing</u>. (plural)

The *-s* on *sings* indicates that it is singular. Do not be confused. Most nouns form their plurals by adding an *-s: chair* becomes *chairs*. Verbs are just the opposite.

The singular and plural forms of the verb are often arranged by *person*. Person indicates the speaker, the person or thing spoken to, or the person or thing spoken about. There are first per-

son, second person, and third person. The *first person* indicates
the person speaking:

(I) will do the assignment.

The *second person* indicates the person or thing spoken to:

(You) should repair the bicycle immediately.

The *third person* indicates the person or thing spoken about:

The (lawnmower) is ready now.

The verb in a sentence must agree in person and number with its
subject, which often is a pronoun. The chart below shows singular
and plural pronouns in the first, second, and third person.

	Pronouns	
Person	*Singular*	*Plural*
First	I, me, my, mine	we, us, our, ours
Second	you, your, yours	you, your, yours
Third	he, him, his,	they, them, their, theirs
	she, her, hers,	
	it, its	

Agreement in Number		
Person	*Singular*	*Plural*
First	I choose	we choose
Second	you choose	you choose
Third	he chooses	they choose

As you can see, the third person singular form of the present tense
verb is the one that ends in *s*. In your writing, do not make needless shifts in person and in number.

> One expects praise when they succeed.
>> *One* is the third person singular *(he, she)*, but *they* is
>> the third person plural. There is a needless shift in
>> number.

> A person should be modest when we are successful.
>> *A person* is the third person singular, but *we* is the

first person plural. There is a needless shift in both person and number.

Mood

Besides having tense, voice, person, and number, verbs are also said to have mood. **The mood indicates the way the speaker views the action or state of the verb.** Is the speaker making a statement of fact, asking a question, or expressing doubt?

There are three moods in English: indicative, imperative, and subjunctive. The *indicative* mood makes a statement or asks a question. It is the most frequently used mood in English.

Ţhe tractor is a John Deere.
The sentence makes a statement.

Is the typewriter an IBM?
The sentence asks a question.

The *imperative* mood gives a command or makes a request.

Open the book!
Open the book, please.

A speaker using the imperative mood is speaking directly to one or more people.

Close the door, John.
The speaker is addressing one person.

Close all books, class.
The speaker is addressing a group of people.

In either case the speaker is addressing the second person—*you*—either singular or plural. Thus it is generally understood that the subject of a verb in the imperative mood is *you*.

(You) open the book.
(You) close the door.

The *subjunctive* mood is the least commonly used mood in English. It reflects doubt, indicates a wish, or expresses a condition contrary to fact.

My wife wishes I <u>were</u> a millionaire.
>The verb *were* follows the indication of a wish.

If I <u>were</u> a millionaire, I would not spend my money foolishly.
>The verb *were* expresses a condition contrary to fact.

Just as with tense, voice, person, and number, you should be careful to avoid needless shifts in mood.

<u>Save</u> your money, and you <u>should buy</u> a house.
>There is a needless shift from the imperative mood to the indicative. Rewrite the sentence to say: *Save* your money and *buy* a house.

If I <u>were</u> a freelance reporter and <u>was</u> not working at a desk eight hours a day, my life would be more interesting.
>There is a needless shift from the subjunctive mood to the indicative. Rewrite the sentence to say: If I *were* a freelance reporter and *were* not working at a desk eight hours a day, my life would be more interesting.

Adverbs

Like adjectives, adverbs are modifiers. Unlike adjectives, which modify nouns and pronouns, however, adverbs modify verbs, adjectives, and other adverbs. As we will see later, adverbs can also modify entire sentences. Adverbs answer the questions How? Where? When? Why? To what extent? and On what condition?

>   v.   adv.
Jackie Joyner-Kersee runs gracefully.
>*Gracefully* is an adverb modifying the verb *runs*. It answers the question *How?* Runs how? gracefully

>   v.   adv.   adv.
Jackie Joyner-Kersee runs very gracefully.
>Now *gracefully* still modifies the verb *runs*, but is itself modified by the adverb *very*. *Very* also answers the question *How?* How gracefully? very gracefully. *Very* modifying *gracefully* is an example of an adverb modifying another adverb.

                    v.   adv.   adj.

Jackie Joyner-Kersee ran an extremely graceful race.
> *Extremely* is an adverb modifying the adjective that
> modifies the noun *race*. How graceful? extremely
> graceful

Now you have examples of adverbs modifying verbs, other adverbs, and adjectives.

Many adverbs, like *extremely* and *gracefully*, end in *-ly*. But many adverbs do not.

                        adv. adv.

Joan Caterman swims quite well.
> Swims how? well (*well* modifies the verb *swims*)
> How well? quite well (*quite* modifies the adverb *well*)

There is the book.
> *There* is an adverb telling where the book is.

Do the assignment now.
> *Now* is an adverb telling when.

Henri will not lie.
> *Not* is an adverb that modifies the verb *will lie* by re-
> stricting its meaning.

In a sentence with the word *cannot*, remember *can* is a verb (auxiliary), but *not* is an adverb.

                v. adv.   v.

Tanya cannot swim.

Prepositions

Prepositions show the position (pre*position*) of one word in relation to another. They are usually short words such as *in, by,* and *to*. Think of a chair, and then think of a preposition as a word that shows the position of various objects in relation to the chair.

> The chair is <u>on</u> the carpet.
> The chair is <u>in</u> the truck.
> The chair is <u>by</u> the fireplace.
> The chair is <u>behind</u> the sofa.

The chair is <u>beside</u> him.
The chair is <u>against</u> the wall.
The chair is <u>near</u> her.

The underlined words are all prepositions. Notice that *carpet, truck, fireplace, sofa, him, wall,* and *her* are all either nouns or pronouns.

A **preposition**, then, **shows the relationship between a noun or pronoun and some other word in the sentence.** The noun or pronoun referred to is generally the one that follows the preposition and is called the object of the preposition.

> n.
>
> That man with the hat always dresses well.
>> *With* is a preposition that shows the relationship be-tween the noun *hat* and the word *man. Hat* is the ob-ject of the preposition *with.*

> n.
>
> The driver crashed through the guardrail.
>> *Through* is a preposition that shows the relationship between the noun *guardrail* and the word *crashed. Guardrail* is the object of the preposition *through.*

> pro.
>
> John gave the book to her.
>> *To* is a preposition that shows the relationship between the pronoun *her* and the word *gave. Her* is the object of the preposition *to.*

Here is a list of words that are commonly used as prepositions.

*according to	before
about	behind
above	below
across	beneath
after	beside
against	besides
along	between
among	beyond
around	**but (when it means *except*)
at	by
*because of	*by means of

despite	*on account of
down	over
during	past
except	till
for	through
from	throughout
in	to
*in addition to	toward
*in back of	under
*in spite of	underneath
*instead of	until
into	up
like	upon
of	with
off	within
on	without

Conjunctions

Conjunctions are connecting words. They connect words and word groups.

Carol and Ted have an ideal relationship.
And connects the words *Carol* and *Ted*.

Either Renée or Barbara will be married by the end of the year.
Either . . . or connects the words *Renée* and *Barbara*.

Eddie will go to the game if it doesn't rain.
If connects *Eddie will go to the game* to *it doesn't rain*.

Conjunctions are classified as either coordinate or subordinate.
Coordinate conjunctions connect words of equal grammatical units.

Maples and oaks are good shade trees.

---

*Multiword prepositions are sometimes called phrasal or group prepositions.
** See pages 34–35.

And connects the equal grammatical units *maples* and *oaks* (noun subjects).

I drove through the city and into the desert.
And connects the equal grammatical units *through the city* and *into the desert* (prepositional phrases).

Alfred loves his dog Pug, but Pug bites him at every opportunity.
But connects the equal grammatical units *Alfred loves his dog Pug* and *Pug bites him at every opportunity* (main clauses).

The coordinate conjunctions are *and, or, but, for, yet, nor,* and sometimes *so. Correlative conjunctions* are coordinate conjunctions that are used in pairs.

My watch is either in the cabinet or on the table.
Either . . . or connects the equal grammatical units *in the cabinet* and *on the table.*

Common correlative conjunctions are *both . . . and, either . . . or, neither . . . nor,* and *not only . . . but also.*
The other type of conjunction is subordinate. The *subordinate conjunction* connects unequal grammatical units (see Chapter 4).

Although I studied diligently, I could not make an A on the test.
Although connects the unequal grammatical units *Although I studied diligently* and *I could not make an A on the test.*

Conjunctions will be explained in more detail in Chapter 4, on clauses. Nevertheless, you may find the following partial list of subordinate conjunctions helpful.

after	as though	since	until
although	because	so that	when
as	before	than	whenever
as if	if	though	wherever
as much as	in order that	unless	while
as long as			

Notice that some subordinate conjunctions can also be prepositions. If such a word introduces a group of related words that
does not contain a subject and a verb, it is a preposition. If it introduces a group of related words that does contain a subject and a
verb, the word is a subordinate conjunction.

> After the dance everyone went home.
>> *After* is a preposition introducing the group of related
>> words not containing a subject and a verb: *after the*
>> *dance.*

> After the dance came to an end, everyone went home.
>> *After* is a subordinate conjunction introducing the
>> group of related words containing a subject and a
>> verb: *After the dance came to an end.*

Interjections

**Interjections are words or groups of words that express
strong emotion.** Although they add little to the meaning of a sentence, they are considered a part of speech. Generally they come
at the beginning of a sentence, but not always.

> Heavens! How could you make such a mess?
>> *Heavens* is an interjection.

> Gee whiz, that is a good paint job.
>> *Gee whiz* is an interjection.

> Damn! That hammer didn't do my finger any good at all.
>> *Damn* is an interjection.

> I'll do the best I can, by golly.
>> *By golly* is an interjection.

Identifying Parts of Speech

You should realize that the part of speech of a word depends on
how the word is used in a sentence. The same word can be one of
several parts of speech, depending on its context or use in a particular sentence. The word *but*, for instance, is commonly used as

a conjunction, as in the sentence *Mary went to the beach, but I stayed home*. On the other hand, the word *but* is a preposition in the sentence *Everyone went to the championship game but me*. Look at these different uses of the word *yellow*:

Yellow is my favorite color. (noun)
Mary has a yellow car. (adjective)
The shirt yellowed in the washing machine. (verb)

Do not be misled into thinking that what you call a preposition in one sentence will always be used as a preposition. When in doubt, consult a dictionary. A good dictionary will classify a word according to the various parts of speech the word can be and give examples of usage.

3

Phrases

A phrase is a group of related words that does not contain a subject and a verb. Phrases also act as particular parts of speech. That is, the words that make up a phrase may act together as one part of speech. For example, in the sentence *José Canseco hit the ball over the fence*, the phrase *over the fence* functions as an adverb because it answers the question Where? The two main types of phrases are prepositional phrases and verbal phrases.

Prepositional Phrases

A prepositional phrase begins with a preposition, ends with the noun or pronoun object, and contains all the modifiers in between, if any. In the earlier phrase *over the fence, over* is the preposition, *fence* is the noun object, and *the* is the modifier. Prepositional phrases almost always function as either adjectives or adverbs.

> The man <u>in the wool suit</u> is uncomfortable.
> *In the wool suit* modifies the noun *man* and is therefore an adjective phrase. Which man?

> There was no game <u>because of the rain</u>.
> *Because of the rain* modifies the verb *was* and is thus an adverb phrase. Why was there no game? because of the rain

Clearly, then, prepositional phrases are groups of related words that do not contain subjects and verbs and that function as adjectives or adverbs.

Verbal Phrases

A verbal is a word that is derived from a verb but that functions as another part of speech. A verbal phrase consists of a verbal and all its modifiers and objects. There are three types of verbals: infinitives, participles, and gerunds.

Infinitives

An infinitive begins with the word *to* and is followed by a verb form.

> To conserve energy is a wise policy.
>> *To conserve* is an infinitive. It begins with the word *to* and is followed by a verb form, *conserve*.

Like verbs, infinitives may have auxiliaries that indicate tense and voice: *to conserve, to have conserved, to be conserved, to have been conserved, to be conserving, to have been conserving.*

> The office building to have been auctioned burned last week.
>> *To have been auctioned* is the present perfect tense, passive voice form of the infinitive.

Infinitives also retain enough verb qualities to take objects.

> The group to present the play is well trained.
>> The infinitive is *to present*. To present what? play. *Play* is the object of the infinitive.

An infinitive phrase consists of the infinitive, its object if it has one, and its modifiers if it has any.

> To elect a qualified president is our goal.
>> *To elect* is the infinitive, *president* is the object of the infinitive, and *a* and *qualified* are modifiers.

One of the modifiers may be another phrase.

> To elect a qualified president for next year is our goal.
>> The prepositional phrase *for next year* is another modifier in the infinitive phrase. Thus, the infinitive phrase contains a prepositional phrase within it.

Infinitive phrases can function as either nouns, adjectives, or adverbs.

To run the mile under 3:50 is every miler's dream.
> *To run the mile under 3:50* is an infinitive phrase used as a noun since it is the subject of the sentence. It answers the question Who or What? asked in front of the verb. Who or what is? to run the mile under 3:50

Notice that the whole phrase functions as a noun. If the sentence read *Speed is every miler's dream,* then the subject would be the one-word noun *speed* rather than the phrase *to run the mile under 3:50*.

As adjective phrases, infinitives usually follow the noun or pronoun they modify.

The obstacle to be overcome is nothing to a man of his ability.
> *To be overcome* is an infinitive phrase used as an adjective modifying the noun *obstacle.* Notice the phrase follows the word it modifies.

Finally, infinitives can function as adverbs.

Jack married the banker's daughter to get a job at the bank.
> *To get a job at the bank* is an infinitive phrase functioning as an adverb. The phrase modifies the verb *married* and answers the question *why.*

Occasionally, infinitives come at the beginning of sentences and modify the whole sentence rather than any particular word in the sentence. Since the most important word in a sentence is generally the verb, however, such infinitive phrases are said to function as adverbs.

To be frank about it, I haven't had any luck with your TV set.
> *To be frank about it* modifies the whole sentence and is therefore considered an infinitive phrase functioning as an adverb.

Participles

Participles are two principal parts of the verb: either the past participle or the present participle. The past participle of the verb is the form that belongs in the blank: I have _____. If the verb is a regular verb, then the past participle will end in *-ed*.

>I have <u>stopped</u>.

If the verb is an irregular verb, then the past participle will end in something other than *-ed*, the most common endings being *-en* or *-t*.

>I have *chosen*.
>I have *slept*.

The present participle of the verb is the form that belongs in the blank: I am _____*ing*. The present participles of both regular and irregular verbs end in *-ing*.

>I am <u>stopping</u>.
>I am <u>sleeping</u>.

Remember, the preceding examples are verbs, not verbals. In the sentences *I have done* and *I am stopping, have done* and *am stopping* are verbs; they express action. To be a verbal, a verb form must function as another part of speech. Participles as verbals must function as adjectives.

>I am working.
>>*Am working* is a verb.

>John Draughn, working in his garden, spotted a rattlesnake.
>>*Working in his garden* is not a verb. *Working* is a verbal functioning as an adjective modifying the noun *John Draughn. Working* is a participle.

In summary, the most common endings of participles are *-ed*, *-en, -t*, and *-ing*. But remember, any verb form that belongs in the blank *I have* _____ can be a participle; thus a few participles will end in something other than *-ed, -en, -t,* or *-ing*.

>I have <u>blown</u>.
>I have <u>done</u>.
>I have <u>rung</u>.

I have <u>heard</u>.

Participles as verbals always function as adjectives. That is all they can ever be. Like infinitives, participles are derived from verbs and therefore can have objects and modifiers. A participial phrase usually begins with a participle, ends with its object, and contains all the modifiers.

<u>Selecting Ann Abrams for the job</u>, the executive feels confident of his choice.
> *Selecting* is the participle, *Ann Abrams* is the object of the participle, and *for the job* is a modifying phrase. The whole participial phrase *selecting Ann Abrams for the job* is used as an adjective modifying the noun *executive*.

Since participles are derived from verbs, they can have different tense forms just as infinitives can.

<u>Having been elected to the board</u>, Carlos was elated.
> The entire participial phrase is underlined. The participle itself is *having been elected*. This is the perfect passive participle form. The whole phrase *having been elected to the board* functions as an adjective modifying the noun *Carlos*.

When participial phrases come at the beginning of sentences, they should modify the first noun or pronoun that comes after the comma that sets off the introductory participial phrase. In the last example, *having been elected to the board* modifies the noun *Carlos*. **Participial phrases that do not modify the first noun or pronoun that follows them are said to be dangling.**

<u>Blowing the litter everywhere</u>, the street was a mess due to the wind.
> *Blowing the litter everywhere* is a participial phrase, but it cannot modify the noun *street*. The street cannot blow the litter around. The sentence should be rewritten to avoid the dangling participle: Blowing the litter everywhere, the wind made a mess of the street.

Participial phrases do not necessarily have to come at the beginning of sentences. When one does not, it will generally come immediately after the noun or pronoun it modifies.

Van Adler is the teller <u>making all the mistakes</u>.
> *Making all the mistakes* is the participial phrase modifying the noun *teller*.

Occasionally, however, participial phrases are tacked on to the end of sentences, far removed from the words they modify. The sentence you just read is an example. *Far removed from the words they modify* is a participial phrase that modifies the noun *phrases*. Here is another example:

The old veteran can be seen every morning, shuffling his feet and hanging his head.
> The two participial phrases *shuffling his feet* and *hanging his head* are tacked on to the end of the sentence and modify *veteran*.

Such sentences can be effective if used sparingly.

Gerunds

The third type of verbal is called a gerund. Gerunds are present participles and thus always end in *-ing*. A gerund always functions as a noun. Though both participles *and* gerunds can end in *-ing*, participles can function only as adjectives and gerunds can function only as nouns.

Like other nouns, gerunds are generally either subjects, direct objects, or objects of prepositions.

<u>Running</u> is a good way to stay trim.
> *Running* is the subject of the verb *is*.

Maria enjoys <u>running</u>.
> *Running* is the direct object of *enjoys*.

Robert Hamstring stays in shape by <u>running</u>.
> *Running* is the object of the preposition *by*.

Like participles and infinitives, gerunds can also take objects and modifiers. A gerund phrase consists of the gerund, its object if there is one, and any modifiers. In the gerund phrase *doing the laundry, doing* is the gerund, *laundry* is the object of the gerund, and *the* is the modifier.

> <u>To shoot accurately</u> is every hunter's desire.
>> *Accurately* is an adverb modifying the infinitive *to shoot*, which is the subject of the verb *is*.

You should not have trouble with participles and gerunds if you remember that participles (which do not always end in *-ing*) are always used as adjectives and that gerunds are always nouns. Remember, the *-ing* verbal could be either a participle or a gerund. Look to see if the verbal is used as an adjective or as a noun. If the verbal ending in *-ing* is not the subject, direct object, or object of a preposition (the most common functions of a noun), it is probably a participle. Also, if a gerund appears at the beginning of a sentence, it is usually the subject of a sentence.

> Getting the car ready for the race was an expensive project.
>> *Getting the car ready for the race* is the subject of the verb *was*.

If a participle comes at the beginning of a sentence, it should modify the first noun or pronoun following the verbal.

> Mowing the lawn every Saturday, John established a ritual for himself.
>> *Mowing the lawn every Saturday* is a participial phrase modifying the noun *John*. *Participial* is the adjective form of the noun participle, and thus the term used to describe this type of phrase.

Notice that a participial phrase appearing at the beginning of a sentence is set off from the main clause with a comma. On the other hand, a gerund at the beginning of a sentence is not generally set off with a comma, because it is undesirable to separate the subject from the verb with a comma.

> Though no technique should be used too often, verbal phrases—especially introductory participial phrases—can make your writing lively.

Without verbal phrase: Elaine is ready to serve the ball and sees her opponent is not in position for a backhand return.

With verbal phrase: Seeing her opponent is not in position for a backhand return, Elaine plans to put her serve in the corner.

Notice how the introductory participial phrase alters the subject-verb pattern and immediately gets the reader's attention with the action word *seeing*.

4

Clauses

In Chapter 2 you learned that conjunctions are connecting words; they connect words and word groups. The two main word groups conjunctions connect are phrases and clauses. Remember that a phrase is a group of related words that does not contain a subject and a verb. *At the man's home* is a phrase, a prepositional phrase. **A clause is a group of related words that does contain a subject and a verb.** *Until the checkered flag was waved* is a clause. The subject is *flag* and the verb is *was waved*. Phrases and clauses can be quite similar, the main difference being that a clause contains a subject and a verb whereas a phrase does not contain either a subject or a verb. Look at the following examples.

Before the dance my date took me out to dinner.

Before the dance began, my date took me out to dinner.

In the first example, *before the dance* is a phrase; it does not contain a subject and a verb. In the second example, *before the dance began* is a clause; it contains the subject *dance* and the verb *began*. The two sentences are similar in meaning, but the structure of the word groups is quite different.

Main Clauses and Subordinate Clauses

There are two types of clauses: main clauses and subordinate clauses. Of course, because they are clauses, both types contain subjects and verbs. A *main clause* expresses a complete thought.

I received an A on my theme.

The sentence contains a subject (*I*) and a verb (*received*) and expresses a complete thought. The main clause *I received an A on my theme* can stand alone. It does not need anything else to complete its meaning.

The other type of clause is a *subordinate clause*. A subordinate clause does not express a complete thought. It depends on a main clause to complete its meaning.

If I were taller, I could play center on the basketball team. *If I were taller* is a subordinate clause. It does not express a complete thought; it cannot stand alone. It depends on the main clause *I could play center on the basketball team* to complete its meaning.

Coordinate conjunctions (*and, or, nor, but, for, yet, so*) can connect only words or word groups of equal rank. Therefore, they can connect two main clauses or two subordinate clauses. They cannot connect a main clause to a subordinate clause because main clauses and subordinate clauses are not of equal rank.

John hid the ring in the attic, but Mary found it. The conjunction *but* connects the main clauses *John hid the ring in the attic* and *Mary found it.*

Whoever is the most dependable and whoever finishes first will receive a bonus. The conjunction *and* connects the two subordinate clauses *whoever is the most dependable* and *whoever finishes first.*

Whoever finishes first and he will receive a bonus. Clearly the sentence is incorrect. A coordinate conjunction cannot connect a subordinate clause (*whoever finishes first*) and a main clause (*he will receive a bonus*).

Subordinate conjunctions, on the other hand, can connect only word groups of unequal rank. In other words, they connect main clauses and subordinate clauses.

Until the project is completed, Barbara will not leave the laboratory. The word *until* subordinates the clause *until the project is completed* and connects it to the main clause *Barbara will not leave the laboratory. Until* is a subordinate conjunction.

Randy made a donation because he felt the money would help.

Because is a subordinate conjunction connecting the subordinate clause *because he felt the money would help* to the main clause *Randy made a donation.*

The following list of words often used as subordinating conjunctions may help you recognize both the conjunctions themselves and the subordinate clauses they introduce:

after	as though	since	until
although	because	so that	when
as	before	than	whenever
as if	if	though	whereas
as much as	in order that	unless	wherever
as long as			while

Good writers often use subordinate clauses to include specific details that qualify or explain a main clause. The most important point is usually stated in the main clause. It is sometimes difficult to tell what a writer's main point is when main clauses and subordinate clauses are used carelessly. Look at the following main clauses.

June wants a lucrative career.
June goes to law school.

If your main point is that June goes to law school, you might say

Since June wants a lucrative career, she is going to law school.

On the other hand, if your main point is that June wants a lucrative career, you might say

June wants a lucrative career when she finishes law school.

Be aware that different subordinate conjunctions can serve different purposes. The subordinate conjunction *because* generally explains *why.*

Why?
Scott walked three miles in a blizzard *because his car broke down.*

The subordinate conjunctions *if* and *unless* answer the question: On what condition?

On what condition?
If you do your homework on Tuesday, you can go to the carnival Wednesday night.

You will not obtain your realtor's license
On what condition?
unless you study for the state licensing examination.

Some subordinate conjunctions tell when an event will occur.

When?
The annual Snow Bowl will be held *when the first snow-flakes fall.*

Clearly, subordinate clauses are useful tools for writers.

More About Subordinate Clauses

Subordinate clauses are sometimes introduced by *relative pronouns* rather than by subordinate conjunctions. A relative pronoun is a pronoun that can connect a subordinate clause to a main clause. A few of the most common relative pronouns are *who, whom, whose, which,* and *that.* Relative pronouns serve much the same function in subordinate clauses as subordinate conjunctions; however, since pronouns can be subjects and objects of verbs whereas conjunctions cannot be, a distinction must be made between the two.

Do the job while you are feeling well.
While is a subordinate conjunction connecting the subordinate clause *while you are feeling well* to the main clause *do the job.*

The man who will win the race must practice constantly.
Who connects the subordinate clause *who will win the race* to the main clause *the man must practice con-*

stantly. However, *who* cannot be considered a subordinate conjunction. A subordinate conjunction cannot be the subject of a verb, but *who* is the subject of the verb *will win.* Thus, *who* is given the special name relative pronoun. The word *who* is a pronoun taking the place of the noun *man.* The sentence literally means *The man (the man will win the race) must practice constantly.*

Relative pronouns eliminate repetition. Look at the following examples.

Without a relative pronoun: Ms. Carr works sixty hours a week. Ms. Carr wants a more responsible position with the company.

With a relative pronoun: Ms. Carr, *who* works sixty hours a week, wants a more responsible position with the company.

Notice that the sentence with the relative pronoun combines two sentences into one and names Ms. Carr only once. As we mentioned, relative pronouns connect subordinate clauses to main clauses. Here, *who works sixty hours a week* is a subordinate clause. Without the main clause, *Ms. Carr wants a more responsible position with the company,* the subordinate clause is incomplete.

Adjective Clauses

Subordinate clauses are like phrases in that they function as either adjectives, adverbs, or nouns. Adjective clauses modify nouns or pronouns and generally follow the words they modify. Adjective clauses are frequently introduced by relative pronouns. Just like one-word adjectives, adjective clauses answer the questions Which one? What kind? How many?

The man who repaired my car graduated from MIT.
Who repaired my car is an adjective clause introduced by the relative pronoun *who,* modifying the noun *man,* and answering the question Which man?

Jackel and Swaim Company has an antique chest that I want.
That I want is an adjective clause introduced by the

relative pronoun *that*, modifying the noun *chest*, and
answering the question Which chest?

It is not unusual, however, to find adjective clauses introduced by
subordinate conjunctions.

Meet me at the bar <u>where we first met</u>.
Where we first met is an adjective clause modifying the
noun *bar*, introduced by the subordinate conjunction
where, and answering the question Which bar?

Adverb Clauses

Adverb clauses modify adjectives, verbs, or other adverbs and are
introduced by subordinate conjunctions such as *where, if, when,
because, although, before*, etc. Like one-word adverbs, adverb
clauses answer the questions How? When? Where? Why? To what
extent? and On what condition?

<u>If I clean the house today</u>, I can play golf this weekend.
If I clean the house today is an adverb clause introduced by the subordinate conjunction *if* and answering the question On what condition?

I could not work the problem <u>because my mind was on
the game</u>.
Because my mind was on the game is an adverb clause
beginning with the subordinate conjunction *because*
and answering the question Why?

Mow the lawn <u>after you go to the grocery store</u>.
After you go to the grocery store is an adverb clause beginning with the subordinate conjunction *after* and answering the question When?

Remember that adjective clauses and adverb clauses are
modifying clauses. That is, they add extra information to clarify
something else. Sentences that contain adjective and adverb
clauses must also contain main clauses. If they did not, the sentences would not express complete thoughts.

If I clean the house today is a subordinate clause; it does not
express a complete thought. On the other hand, *The man gradu-*

ated from MIT, Jackel and Swaim Company has an antique chest, and *I can play golf this weekend* are all sentences, expressing complete thoughts. Notice that modifying clauses can be omitted from sentences and the sentences still express complete thoughts. Another thing to remember in studying subordinate clauses is that the whole clause works as one word.

> The <u>black</u> car needs a good coating of wax.
> *Black* is a one-word adjective describing *car.*

> The car <u>that is painted black</u> needs a good coating of wax.
> *That is painted black* is an adjective clause modifying the noun *car.*

In analyzing the subordinate clause, though, you cannot say Which car? *black* car. You must say Which car? the one *that is painted black.* The words in a subordinate clause are a unit. You cannot separate the words and have the separated words modify the main clause. Again, you must consider the group of related words in the subordinate clause as one word.

Also, in studying clauses, do not be surprised to find phrases and clauses that seem to do the same thing.

> The man <u>reading the road map</u> is lost.
> The man <u>who is reading the road map</u> is lost.

The first sentence contains the participial phrase *reading the road map* which modifies the noun *man.* The second sentence contains the adjective clause *who is reading the road map* which modifies the noun *man.* Both the phrase and the clause do the same thing. The difference between them is grammatical. The phrase does not contain a subject and a verb, and the clause does. Sometimes different grammatical constructions can communicate the same meaning. This choice of different ways to say the same thing gives language flexibility and variety.

Noun Clauses

Noun clauses are usually introduced by relative pronouns.

> John knows <u>who will win the race this year.</u>
> *Who will win the race this year* is a noun clause. It is

the direct object of the verb *knows* and is introduced by the relative pronoun *who*.

Nouns, unlike adjectives and adverbs, are not modifiers. They are naming words. Nouns commonly function as subjects, direct objects, objects of prepositions, and predicate nominatives, though they can have other functions too. The point that you must remember, however, is that nouns are more important in sentences than adjectives and adverbs. If you take a noun clause out of a sentence, the sentence will no longer stand on its own.

<u>Whoever completes the assignment first</u> wins the cheesecake.
>*Whoever completes the assignment first* cannot be left out of the sentence without destroying the meaning. *Wins the cheesecake* cannot stand on its own. It is not a main clause because it does not contain a subject and therefore cannot express a complete thought.

Adjectives and adverbs can be removed from a sentence just as your tonsils and your appendix can be removed from your body. Without adjectives and adverbs the sentence can still function, although the meaning of the sentence may be altered. For example, *The boys who wear white socks are spurned by the girls* implies a different meaning than *The boys are spurned by the girls*. *Who wear white socks* is an essential adjective clause because it is essential to the meaning of the sentence. The girls do not spurn all the boys, only those who wear white socks. Nevertheless, whether the sentence contains the adjective clause or not, it still functions and still makes sense. On the other hand, if a noun clause is removed from a sentence, the sentence can no longer function, just as your car could no longer function if the engine were removed.

Remember the importance of a noun clause to a sentence, or you will not always be able to recognize a complex sentence. A complex sentence contains one main clause and at least one subordinate clause. (See Chapter 5 for more on complex sentences.) When the subordinate clause is an adjective clause, the main clause still makes sense without it:

Adjective: Anna gave Phil, who is her neighbor's husband, a gold ring.
>With the adjective clause *who is her neighbor's hus-*

band omitted, the main clause still expresses a complete thought, *Anna gave Phil a gold ring.*

When an adverb clause is omitted from a sentence, the main clause that is left can stand alone.

Adverb: I would like to finish the novel before I mow the lawn.

With *before I mow the lawn* omitted, the main clause still expresses a complete thought, *I would like to finish the novel.*

The sentences containing the adjective clause and the adverb clause are complex sentences. Each sentence contains one main clause and one subordinate clause.

The sentence you read earlier containing a noun clause is also a complex sentence.

Whoever completes the assignment first wins the cheesecake.

In this sentence the subordinate clause is the noun clause *whoever completes the assignment first*, which functions as the subject. The main clause is the whole sentence. Thus the sentence is a complex sentence containing one main clause and one subordinate clause. When the subordinate clause is a noun clause, it is so important to the main clause that it is inherently part of the main clause itself. If you put the subordinate clause in brackets and underline the main clause, the sample sentence looks like this:

[Whoever completes the assignment first] wins the cheesecake.

Notice what happens if the subordinate clause is a noun clause functioning as the object of a preposition.

Give the lab report to [whoever is on duty.]

The main clause would be left hanging at the word *to* without an object for the preposition if the subordinate noun clause were omitted. Notice again that the subordinate clause is a group of related words functioning as one word. If the sentence had read, *Give the lab report to Dr. Smith*, then *Dr. Smith* would have been the object of the preposition *to*. Now, however, instead of just one person's name you have a clause (*whoever is on duty*) functioning as the object of the preposition. The principle is the same.

Since noun clauses generally function as subjects, direct objects, objects of prepositions, or predicate nominatives, you may find it helpful to study examples of each.

Subject: Whoever shoots an arrow through the axe handles will win Penelope's hand.

Direct object: I think that Sam Brame is the best-dressed man in town.

Object of preposition: The boss is saving the gold drafting set for whoever produces the best design.

Predicate nominative: The job is what Greg needs.

Misplaced Subordinate Clauses

Effectively using subordinate clauses can improve your writing. But an improper use of subordinate clauses can confuse, if not amuse, your reader. You must make sure that adjective clauses are placed near the words they modify.

The book belongs to the young student that contains 300 pages of color reproductions.
As stated, the student contains 300 pages of color reproductions.

The sentence should have been written so that the adjective clause *that contains 300 pages of color reproductions* was placed nearer the word it modifies:

The book that contains 300 pages of color reproductions belongs to the young student.

John Fergusson bought a tractor from a local farmer that runs on diesel fuel.

A sentence like this would amuse your reader—at your expense. The adjective clause should be placed nearer the word *tractor*:

John Fergusson bought a tractor that runs on diesel fuel from a local farmer.

5

Sentence Types and Sentence Variety

In order to give your writing variety, you will need to use the four types of sentences: simple, compound, complex, and compound-complex. These sentence types are summarized in the following chart.

Sentence Types	Main Clauses	Subordinate Clauses
Simple	1	0
Compound	2 or more	0
Complex	1	1 or more
Compound-Complex	2 or more	1 or more

Later in this chapter, you will learn how to use your knowledge of sentence types to write more effective sentences through the use of sentence variety, parallelism, and the control of excessive main clauses and subordination.

Sentence Types

Simple Sentences

A simple sentence contains one main clause. That is, it contains one subject and one verb and expresses a complete thought.

> s.   v.
> *Anne has become* a successful lawyer.

This is a simple sentence. An imperative command can also be a simple sentence.

> Hush!

Hush! is a simple sentence. The subject *you* is understood, and the single word expresses a complete thought. Simple sentences can also have compound subjects.

> John, Ted, Bob, Alice, and Sheila went to the country fair.
> The subject is compounded five times. Grammatically, however, it still has only one subject and one verb, and thus is a simple sentence. Similarly, the verb can be compounded.

> Shirley cleaned the house, washed her dress, and went to dinner at Delmonico's.
> The verb is compounded three times, but the sentence is still a simple sentence. It contains several verbs, which all have the same subject.

And, of course, a simple sentence can contain a compound subject and a compound verb.

> John, Mary, Ted, Susan, Greg, and Peggy went to dinner, danced until 8:00, and saw a play at the local theater.
> This sentence is still just a simple sentence. It contains only one verb and one subject. The same group of nouns is the subject of the same group of verbs.

Remember when studying sentence types that you are counting only clauses. All you have to do is learn the four types of sentences and then count the number of main and subordinate clauses in a sentence to see which type of sentence you have. But only clauses count.

> By hanging on to the window ledge, Barbara was able to escape the fire in her room.
> *Hanging on to the window ledge* is a participial phrase and *to escape the fire in her room* is an infinitive phrase, but the sentence is a simple sentence because it contains only one verb *was* and one subject *Barbara*. The whole sentence, of course, expresses a complete thought. Do not be misled by considering verbal phrases as subordinate clauses. Remember, phrases do not contain subjects and verbs.

Compound Sentences

A compound sentence contains two or more main clauses and no subordinate clauses. You might think of a compound sentence as two or more simple sentences put into one sentence. The main clauses of a compound sentence can be joined in two ways. They may be joined by a semicolon:

> In some ways transformational grammar is easier than traditional grammar; transformational grammar uses fewer terms.

They may be joined by a comma and a coordinate conjunction (*and, or, nor, for, but, yet, so*).

> In some ways transformational grammar is easier than traditional grammar, but most students prefer the traditional approach.

Remember that a compound sentence can be composed of more than two main clauses. It can have as many main clauses as you can think up, as long as it contains no subordinate clauses.

> In some ways transformational grammar is easier than traditional grammar, but most students prefer the traditional method; they are more comfortable with the vocabulary of traditional grammar, and they are hesitant to face a new way of studying the language.

That compound sentence contains four main clauses and no subordinate clauses.

First main clause:	In some ways transformational grammar is easier than traditional grammar,
Second main clause:	but most students prefer the traditional method;
Third main clause:	they are more comfortable with the vocabulary of traditional grammar,
Fourth main clause:	and they are hesitant to face a new way of studying the language.

The first and second main clauses are joined by a comma and the coordinate conjunction *but*. The second and third main clauses are joined by a semicolon. The third and fourth main clauses are joined by a comma and the coordinate conjunction *and*.

As you have seen, compound sentences connect main clauses. However, the main clauses they connect should relate to each other logically. For example, a sentence such as *James Comer is a strong Democrat, and Lassie has fleas* is ridiculous. Though grammatically correct, the sentence contains two main clauses that are not logically related.

Complex Sentences

A complex sentence has one main clause and one or more subordinate clauses.

> [After I read the article], I disagreed with the author even more than before.
>> *After I read the article* is an introductory adverb clause. *I disagreed with the author even more than before* is a main clause. The sentence is complex.

> The man [who wins the most primaries] will receive the nomination in Philadelphia [where the convention is to be held].
>> The above sentence has one main clause (underlined) and two subordinate clauses (bracketed), so it is a complex sentence. (See pp. 115–116.)

Remember from the preceding chapter, however, that noun clauses are different from modifying clauses. With noun clauses the subordinate clause will be an integral part of the main clause.

> [Whoever wins the primaries] will go to Philadelphia.
>> *Whoever wins the primaries* is a noun clause, subject of the verb *will go*. The main clause is the whole sentence *Whoever wins the primaries will go to Philadelphia*. You must consider the noun clause subject to be an integral part of the main clause; obviously *will go to Philadelphia* could not be a main clause since it nei-

ther contains a subject nor expresses a complete thought. The whole sentence is a complex sentence.

You should realize that some subordinate clauses functioning as adjectives and nouns may omit the relative pronouns ordinarily used to connect the subordinate clause to the main clause.

A 1956 Thunderbird is the car I want.
> *I want* is an adjective clause modifying the noun *car*. The sentence could be written with the relative pronoun included: A 1956 Thunderbird is the car *that I want*.

The same situation occurs with noun clauses.

The man at the nursery knows I want the pink azalea.
> *I want the pink azalea* is a noun clause that functions as the direct object of the verb *knows*.

The sentence could be written this way:

The man at the nursery knows *that I want the pink azalea*.

Both sentences are complex sentences whether the relative pronoun is present or not.

Remember, a clause is a group of related words that contains a subject and a verb. Every time you find a different verb that takes its own subject, you have another clause. In the sentence *The man at the nursery knows I want the pink azalea*, you should recognize that *man* is the subject of the verb *knows* and that *I* is the subject of the verb *want*.

Compound-Complex Sentences

A compound-complex sentence contains two or more main clauses and one or more subordinate clauses.

I wanted to go to the outdoor concert, but I had to change my plans since my lab report is due by 5:00 P.M.
> *I wanted to go to the outdoor concert* is a main clause; *but I had to change my plans* is a main clause; *since my lab report is due by 5:00 P.M.* is a subordinate adverb clause telling why or on what condition.

Here the main clauses are underlined and the subordinate clauses are in brackets:

> I wanted to go to the outdoor concert, but I had to change my plans [since my lab report is due by 5:00 P.M.]

Look at the following sentence:

> [When the plants started producing,] we noticed a problem [because many of the tomatoes had rotten spots on the bottom;] we called a botanist, and he told us the solution.

Notice that the sentence contains three main clauses and two subordinate clauses. The sentence is compound-complex.

Do not forget that some of your subordinate clauses in compound-complex sentences may be noun clauses.

> noun clause
> I know [what you want to hear], so you are not going to be disappointed.

Also, you must remember that some of the relative pronouns may be omitted in compound-complex sentences just as they were in complex sentences.

> Dr. Smith said [you performed well], but he told me [you had some trouble with a chapter] [you had worked on the week before].
>> *You performed well* is a noun clause direct object; the relative pronoun *that* is omitted. *You had some trouble with a chapter* is a noun clause direct object; again the relative pronoun *that* is omitted. *You had worked on the week before* is a subordinate adjective clause modifying *chapter;* the relative pronoun *(that)* is omitted.

Sentence Variety and Improvement

Sentence Variety

Good writing contains a variety of sentence structures and types. It will have introductory phrases and clauses sometimes, short simple sentences sometimes, and long, involved compound-complex sentences sometimes; occasionally good writing will have a compound sentence or two, though compound sentences are perhaps the least used of the four types.

> Denise wanted to buy a 1978 Volkswagen convertible. She knew it was a classic. She was not sure she could afford the price the owner asked. Seven thousand dollars seemed like too much. She considered offering $6,000. She really thought $5,000 or $5,500 was more reasonable. She knew the car had to be hers. She test drove it and offered $5,300. There was some negotiating. Denise and the owner settled on a price of $6,000. The owner wanted more. Denise felt it was too much. But now Denise is the proud owner.

The paragraph is rather dull and choppy. It lacks variety and a smooth flow. Now read the revised version of the paragraph and see the difference:

> Although Denise knew the 1978 Volkswagen convertible was a classic, she was not sure she could afford the price asked by the owner. Thinking $7,000 was too much, she considered offering $6,000. In her mind she felt $5,000 or $5,500 was a more reasonable price, but in her heart she knew the car had to be hers. She test drove it and offered $5,300. After some negotiation, Denise and the owner settled on a purchase price of $6,000. The owner felt she should have gotten more, and Denise felt she paid too much. However, Denise is the proud owner of a classic automobile.

The revised version has more complex sentences. If used skillfully, complex sentences and compound-complex sentences can communicate more information in fewer sentences and with a smoother flow than simple sentences and compound sentences. If you are conscious of varying your sentence patterns when you write, you can greatly improve your writing. There are, however, other techniques besides varying sentence types.

1. Begin sentences with participial phrases.

> Bob loves Cheryl deeply, and he proposed to her last Friday night.

The sentence is grammatically correct. But look what happens when the sentence is rewritten with an introductory participial phrase:

> Loving Cheryl deeply, Bob proposed to her last Friday night.

The verbal quality of *loving* immediately gets the reader's attention. Also, the sentence has a little more suspense since the reader has to wait longer before coming to the main part of the sentence.

2. Begin some sentences with introductory adverb clauses.

> The championship game was canceled due to rain. Everyone stayed in the dorm.

The two sentences do not even seem to belong together. But by using an introductory adverb clause, the two sentences become one sentence.

> Since the championship game was canceled due to rain, everyone stayed in the dorm.

Sentence variety can be improved somewhat just by using an adverb or adverbs at the beginning of the sentence.

> Interestingly enough, everyone stayed in the dorm.

Interestingly enough is an adverbial expression. Since it does not modify any particular word in the sentence, it is known as an absolute construction. The expression just used is called an adverb absolute. Be sure not to overuse the adverb absolute construction; it is merely a technique for achieving variety and is not necessarily beneficial or detrimental. Some readers do not like adverb absolutes like *interestingly* and *hopefully*. Author and commentator Edwin Newman has a sign over his office door that reads, "Abandon *hopefully*, all ye that enter here."

Parallelism

Another way to improve your sentence structure is by the effective use of parallelism. Parallelism is the similarity of grammatical form between two or more elements that serve the same function. The underlying principle of parallelism is that in a series nouns should be balanced with nouns, verbs with verbs, adjectives with adjectives, infinitive phrases with infinitive phrases, etc. In the sentence *I have an apple, an orange, and a tomato,* the words *an* before *apple, an* before *orange,* and *a* before *tomato* illustrate the correct parallel use of words. The sentence *I bought an apple, orange, and a tomato* is not parallel. The word *an* appears before the word *apple* and *a* appears before *tomato;* but since there is no adjective before the word *orange,* the series is not parallel. Errors of this kind are known as faulty parallelism. Such errors can be distracting to readers. Notice the faulty parallelism in the following sentence: *This summer I want to get plenty of rest, to attend summer school, and play golf.* As is often the case, the faulty parallelism can be corrected in more than one way. The sign of the infinitive *(to)* can be added before *play golf: This summer I want to get plenty of rest, to attend summer school, and to play golf.* Or the sign of the infinitive may be given just once, making the other two phrases parallel with the word *to: This summer I want to get plenty of rest, attend summer school, and play golf.* The second way is preferable because fewer words are used to achieve equal clarity.

Phrases are parallel when infinitives are paired with infinitives and gerunds are paired with gerunds.

Parallel: Jack wants to be elected chairman and to set up a new finance committee.

The infinitive phrases *to be elected chairman* and *to set up a new finance committee* are parallel.

Parallel: Dawn likes riding horses and playing tennis.

The two gerund phrases *riding horses* and *playing tennis* are parallel.

Faulty parallelism arises when phrases are not in the same grammatical form.

Not parallel: Dawn likes riding horses and to play tennis. The gerund phrase *riding horses* is not grammatically equal to the infinitive phrase *to play tennis.*

Parallel subordinate clauses repeat the relative pronouns that introduce them.

Parallel: Kurt knows that he will get the job and that he will be good at it.
The subordinate clauses *that he will get the job* and *that he will be good at it* are parallel because both are introduced by the relative pronoun *that* and both are objects of the verb *knows.*

When one of the relative pronouns is omitted, the sentence is confusing.

Not parallel: Kurt knows that he will get the job and he will be good at it.

Sometimes entire sentences are parallel (or balanced).

Parallel: The country will move ahead with the administration's new programs. The citizens will move ahead with the country.

Parallel sentences are often used in speeches because they are dramatic and effective. However, too many parallel sentences in writing may seem repetitious.
In your writing be sure the elements you connect are parallel.

Not parallel: Joan runs to lose weight, for exercise, and because she enjoys running.
The sentence connects an infinitive phrase (*to lose weight*), a prepositional phrase (*for exercise*), and an adverb clause (*because she enjoys running*). The sentence can be made parallel by making all the elements grammatically equal.

Parallel: Joan runs because she loses weight, gets exercise, and enjoys running.

Not parallel: We can improve ourselves by setting goals and determination.

Parallel: We can improve ourselves by setting goals and having determination.

Not parallel: Whether in a crowd or when he was alone, Conrad was always the same.

Parallel: Whether alone or in a crowd, Conrad was always the same.

Not parallel: Irving Smith is a man with a muscular build and who attends a health spa every week.

Parallel: Irving Smith is a man who has a muscular build and (or *who*) attends a health spa every week.

Avoiding Excessive Main Clauses

Too many main clauses in a row result in choppy and distracting writing. The Tom, Dick, and Jane books students once learned to read in elementary school are an example of how too many simple sentences cause choppiness.

Tom has a sister. His sister is Jane. Tom and Jane have a neighbor. The neighbor is Dick. Dick has a dog. The dog is Spot.

If it were not for the excitement of learning to read, children would have a difficult time enduring many such sentences. Compound sentences can be equally choppy when you merely string together a lot of main clauses in one sentence.

I really like to go bowling on Friday nights, and I am pretty good, and I might make the all-star team, but I don't know many people at the bowling lanes, and I need to know the judges selecting the all-stars.

You can avoid such strung-out compound sentences by subordinating some of the clauses, by using compound verbs, by using phrases, and by rewriting the one sentence into two or more sentences.

I enjoy my Friday night bowling and bowl pretty well. By getting to know more people at the bowling lanes, I would have a good chance of making the all-star team. A prospect must know the judges.

The long, stringy sentence has now become three sentences. There is greater variety, the paragraph is easier to read, and the essential information is not altered.

Avoiding Excessive Subordination

Mark Twain once wrote a story about an old man who tried to tell a story about a ram. Unfortunately, the narrator got so bogged down in details that the story never got told. Whenever the narrator thought of another character, he gave so much of the character's genealogy that he forgot the character's significance to the story. The reader never does learn anything about the ram; the narrator went to sleep before completing his tale. Your writing can get bogged down in details, too, if you subordinate excessively.

Look at the following sentence:

> The man who is now my next-door neighbor recently bought himself a new car that is so big it won't fit into his garage that was built by the previous owner of the house who owned a Volkswagen.

The sentence is grammatically correct, but it sounds as though it is continually running downhill. The only cure for a sentence like this is to rewrite it, rearranging the details and perhaps leaving some of them out.

> The garage, having been built for the previous owner's Volkswagen, could not accommodate my neighbor's new car.

The sentence is even more effective if shorter still.

> The garage built for the previous owner's Volkswagen could not accommodate my neighbor's new car.

6

Agreement

Subject-Verb Agreement

The main thing to remember about subject-verb agreement is that the subject must agree with the verb in number. If the subject is singular, the verb should be singular; if the subject is plural, the verb should be plural. You do not want to commit errors in agreement. Though agreement errors are not serious barriers to communication, they often create social barriers.

Errors in agreement are easy to correct. By careful proofreading, you could probably identify all such errors. Nevertheless, it is not surprising that many people make careless slips. Children just learning the language know that the plural of *boy* is formed by adding an *-s*. They consider it only logical that the verb should also have an *-s*, so they say *The boys shows their rocks*. Unfortunately, the English language is not so conveniently logical. In English most nouns do form their plurals by adding an *-s*.

Singular	add *-s*	*Plural*
house		houses
desk		desks
book		books
phone		phones

But verbs do not form their plurals in the same way. Look at the following conjugation:

Singular	*Plural*
I look	we look
you look	you look
he, she, it looks	they look

Notice that the form of the verb that ends in -*s* is singular, not plural. It is the third person singular form of the verb that ends in -*s*.

Singular	remove -*s*	*Plural*
runs		run
throws		throw
jumps		jump

Notice, also, that only the present tense presents a problem. If a verb is in the past tense, for example, there is no -*s* form.

I looked	we looked
you looked	you looked
he, she, it looked	they looked

Remember the basic rule of subject-verb agreement: the subject must agree with the verb in number.

The boy looks.
>The word *boy* is a singular noun, so it takes the singular form of the verb *(looks)*.

The boys look.
>The word *boys* is plural, so the verb *(look)* is plural.

Beware of the following situations concerning subject-verb agreement, so you can avoid awkward choices in your writing.

1.   Words having an *s* in the last syllable can be misleading.

The scientist studies the problem every day.
>*Scientist* is singular because it does not end in -*s*. The verb correctly takes the singular form. If you are not careful, however, you will hear the *s* in *scientist* and consider it plural and commit the following error:

The scientist study the problem every day.
>*Scientist* is singular, but the verb *study* is plural; the subject and verb do not agree in number.

The verb can also have an *s* sound.

> Quarterbacks risk their careers every time they are tackled. *Risk* is a verb with an *s* sound, but it does not end in -*s*. You must realize that the verb is plural as it is and thus is correctly used with the plural *quarterbacks*. The following error is easy to make.

> The quarterback risk his career every time he is tackled. Now the verb *risk* has an *s* sound, and it almost sounds correctly used. However, the third person *quarterback* is a singular noun and should have a third person singular verb, which is the verb form ending in -*s*.

> The quarterback risks his career every time he is tackled.

Sometimes both the subject and the verb end in *s* sounds.

> The scientist exists to work and to learn. Now both the subject *scientist* and the verb *exists* end in -*s* sounds. But since the subject is singular and does not end in -*s* and since the verb is singular and does end in -*s*, the subject and verb agree in number.

2.   Some people tend to reverse the basic rule that subject and verb should agree in number.

> **Nonstandard:** Bob do very well when given enough time.
> **Standard:** Bob does very well when given enough time.

In the first sentence *Bob* is the singular subject, but the verb is the plural *do;* the subject and verb do not agree in number.

In the second sentence *Bob* is the singular subject and *does* is the singular verb; the subject and verb agree in number. Try to avoid writing sentences like the first example.

> **Nonstandard:** The girls goes to a square dance every Saturday night.
> **Standard:** The girls go to a square dance every Saturday night.

The subject and verb do not agree in the first sentence because the subject *girls* is plural but the verb *goes* is singular. There is agreement between the subject and verb of the second example, however. The subject *girls* and the verb *go* are both plural.

3. Words and phrases coming between the subject and the verb can be misleading.

> The statues in the park on Main Street are beautiful.
> *Statues* is the subject, and since it is plural, it takes the plural form of the verb *are*. *Park* and *street* are singular, but they are objects of prepositions, not part of the subject.

> John, as well as several other men, loves Mary.
> Even though the word *men* comes between the subject *John* and the verb *loves*, the sentence still must have a singular verb agreeing with the singular subject.

Similarly, if the subject were plural, the verb would be plural:

> Several men, including John, love Mary.
> The plural subject *men* is not affected by the expression *including John* and therefore the verb is correctly plural, *love*.

4. Subjects connected by *and* are generally plural. That two subjects joined by *and* are plural should be obvious: one plus one equals two.

> Bud and Roscoe are fine men.
> *Bud* is singular; *Roscoe* is singular—but together they are two men, and thus the subject is plural and needs a plural verb, *are*.

Of course, there may be more than two singular subjects joined by *and:*

> Mark Twain, Henry James, Nathaniel Hawthorne, Herman Melville, and William Faulkner are just a few of America's well-known authors.
> Though each author is an individual, together the five authors make up the plural subject that needs the plural verb, *are*.

Sometimes the two "subjects" joined by *and* may relate to the same person or thing.

> My best friend and adviser is my wife.
>> *Friend* and *adviser* both mean the same person and thus the verb is singular, *is*. Such sentences do not cause much confusion because the meaning is normally clear.

> Ham and eggs is a good dish.
>> Though there are two separate nouns joined by *and*, the verb is singular *(is)* because *ham and eggs* refers to one particular dish.

5. Indefinite pronouns are sometimes treated as singular and sometimes as plural. Indefinite pronouns such as *another, anyone, anybody, anything, each, either, everyone, everybody, everything, neither, no one, nobody, nothing, one, someone, somebody, something* are grammatically considered to be singular in formal English.

> Everyone on the team performs well.
>> Though the word *everyone* seems to indicate more than one person, the word is an indefinite pronoun that is considered to be grammatically singular, and thus *everyone* takes the singular form of the verb, *performs.*

Remember, grammar organizes the way language is used; grammar is not necessarily logical because language is not necessarily logical. You say, "The trousers are hanging on the line," even though the noun *trousers* indicates only one (singular) garment.

> Each of the women puts in as much time as she can on the project.
>> *Each* is an indefinite pronoun considered to be singular, so it takes the singular verb *puts.*

Indefinite pronouns such as *several, both,* and *many* are plural when used as subjects.

> Both of the men are in the race.
>> *Both* is clearly plural, and therefore the verb is plural.

Several of the runners have as many as five pairs of track shoes.
> *Several* is plural and takes the plural verb *have*.

Indefinite pronouns such as *none* and *some* can be either singular or plural depending on meaning.

Some of the gold was pure.
> The word *some* is used in a singular sense to indicate one particular portion and takes the singular verb.

Some of the men were exhausted after the workday ended.
> *Some* is used as an indefinite pronoun like *several, both,* and *many.* It clearly means more than one of the men and therefore takes the plural verb.

None of that money is mine.

None of the applicants were hired.

6.   Singular subjects connected by *or, nor, either . . . or,* or *neither . . . nor* need a singular verb because either choice would be singular. For example,

Either Blanca or Larry is going to be appointed to the position.
> If Blanca is chosen, the subject is singular. If Larry is chosen, the subject is singular. Therefore, the verb in either case would be singular, *is going.*

The same situation would exist with *neither . . . nor:*

Neither Blanca nor Larry is going to be appointed to the position.

Be careful, however, when one of the subjects is singular and one is plural. The verb must agree with the subject nearer the verb.

Neither the employees nor the owner has control over the strike.
> The singular subject *owner* is nearer the verb, and thus the singular form of the verb *(has)* is used.

Neither the owner nor the employees have control over
the strike.
Now the plural subject *employees* is nearer the verb,
so the correct verb form is the plural *have*.

7. Sentences that have the verb preceding the subject require
special attention. Many sentences beginning with prepositional
phrases can be confusing.

Off the northwest coast of Scotland are the Western Isles.
The subject is the plural *Western Isles.* Don't let the
singular *coast* or the singular *Scotland* confuse you;
both are objects of prepositions. Since the subject is
the plural *Western Isles,* the verb is the plural *are.*

Sentences beginning with *there is* or *there are* alter the ordinary
subject-verb order.

There is only one man working on the pump.
The subject is *man,* and that is why the verb is singular.

There are three hundred men working on the reactor.
This time the subject is the plural *men,* so the verb is
the plural *are.*

In speech, especially, you have to be careful with *there is* or *there
are* sentences since you have to choose your verb before you state
your subject. In writing, you should avoid sentences beginning
with *there is* and *there are.*

8. Nouns such as *family, jury, council, group, committee, board,
faculty,* and the like may be considered either singular or plural
depending on meaning.
A word such as *family* is known as a collective noun. It can
represent either one collective unit or the plural components of
the unit.

A family is not as close a social unit as it used to be.
The noun *family* refers to a collective unit (one
group), and therefore the singular verb *is* must be
used with the singular subject.

The family have to plan their activities for the week.
> In this sentence *family* is a plural word because it re-
fers to the members of the group as several individu-
als, thus the plural verb, *have.*

The jury is returning to the courtroom.
> The subject *jury* is a collective unit and therefore
singular.

The jury are arguing among themselves.
> The word *jury* is referring to twelve people as individu-
als and is therefore plural.

In general usage *the number* (meaning one particular number) is considered singular whereas *a number* (meaning some) is
considered plural. The difference between *a number* and *the number* stems from the difference between the general article *a* and
the definite article *the,* a difference most people never notice. If
you say *a monkey,* you are referring to any monkey; whereas if you
say *the monkey,* you are referring to a particular one.

The number of Phi Beta Kappa students is small.

A number of students are going to the game.

9.   A relative pronoun used as a subject may take either a singular verb or a plural verb depending on the pronoun's antecedent.
(Relative pronouns are words such as *who, whom, whose, which,*
and *that* that serve as both pronouns and subordinators—as in the
sentence *The man who receives the trophy must win the race by at
least one lap.*)
Remember that an antecedent is the noun a pronoun takes
the place of. If the antecedent of a relative pronoun is singular, the
pronoun must take a singular verb.

> sing.   sing.
One problem   ←(that)→   arises in nuclear reactors is excessive heat.
>> *That* is a relative pronoun; its antecedent is the singu-
lar noun *problem.* Therefore, the verb *arises* must be
singular to agree with its singular subject *that.*

pl.   pl.

People ←(who)→ go down into the mines have courage.

> *People* is plural, *who* is plural; the verb *go* must be plural to agree with the word *who*.

He is one of those workers who want the best possible product.

> In this sentence the antecedent of *who* is the plural noun *workers;* thus the plural form of the verb *(want)* is used.

10.   Gerund subjects take singular verbs. A gerund is a verbal that ends in *-ing* and functions as a noun. When the subject of a sentence is a gerund, use a singular verb.

Seeing all of Shakespeare's history plays performed was his goal.

> *Seeing* is the gerund subject so the singular form of the verb *(was)* is used.

Playing tennis once a week is a good way to get the exercise your body needs.

> *Playing* is the singular gerund subject of the singular verb *is*.

11.   Some nouns are grammatically singular though they end in *-s*. Quite a few nouns are plural in form (end in *-s*) but singular in meaning. Words such as *news, physics, economics, aeronautics, athletics, aesthetics,* and *measles* are all singular nouns. These nouns should cause you little if any confusion because you never hear them in any other form.

sing. sing.

The news is all bad this evening.

sing. sing.

Measles is a disease potentially dangerous to some people.

Many book, magazine, and newspaper titles end in *-s* but take singular verbs. Such a title is singular because it indicates the name of only one book, magazine, or newspaper.

The Complete Grimm's Fairy Tales is a fascinating collection of stories for young and old.

> Though the last word in the title is a noun ending in -*s* (*Tales*), the verb must be singular (*is*). After all, *The Complete Grimm's Fairy Tales* is only one title of one book.

          sing.   sing.

The New York Times leads all American newspapers in sales.

Pronoun-Antecedent Agreement

Pronouns and their antecedents must agree in number just as subjects and verbs do. Many of the same principles apply because the situations are similar. When an antecedent is singular, the pronoun referring to it should be singular; when an antecedent is plural, the pronoun referring to it should be plural.

1. A singular pronoun is used to refer to such words as *another, anyone, anybody, each, either, everyone, everybody, kind, man, woman, neither, no one, nobody, one, person, someone, somebody, sort,* and *type.*

A person must do her work on time.

> *Person* is the singular antecedent of the singular pronoun *her*. The pronoun and its antecedent are both singular and therefore agree in number.

The woman worked all Friday night preparing for the yard sale she was to have on Saturday.

> *Woman* is the singular antecedent of the singular pronoun *she*. The pronoun and its antecedent are in agreement.

Anyone can learn English grammar if he studies hard enough.

> *Anyone* is an indefinite pronoun considered to be singular. The singular pronoun *he* refers to the singular *anyone*, so pronouns and antecedent agree.

Even though many television commercials say things like "Everyone in today's chaotic world feels free to do their own thing," traditional usage requires a singular pronoun in place of the plural *their*. When the gender is in doubt, some writers prefer to use the *he or she* form:

> Any student may do the extra credit project if he or she feels it will be beneficial.

Since it is distracting to have a proliferation of *he or she's* in a paper (as in the sentence *Every man or woman should do his or her own thing as he or she sees fit*), the problem can be avoided by using a plural subject and the pronoun *their:*

> Today's students feel free to pursue their own interests.

Words such as *kind, type,* and *sort* require special attention when they are used with the adjectival pronouns *this* and *these, that* and *those.*

> These kind are generally preferred.
> > *These* is plural, and *kind* is singular. The sentence should read:
>
> This kind is generally preferred.
> > or
>
> These kinds are generally preferred.
>
> Those type of inventions never work efficiently.
> > *Those* is plural, and *type* is singular. The sentence should read:
>
> This type of invention never works efficiently.
> > or
>
> Those types of inventions never work efficiently.

2.   Two or more antecedents joined by *and* are referred to by a plural pronoun.

> Hugh and Jimmy do all they can to maintain the building.
> > *Hugh* and *Jimmy* become plural by being connected with the conjunction *and;* therefore, the plural *they* is needed so the antecedents and pronoun will agree.

The buildings to be destroyed were the Kingsmore Building, the Avondale Tower, and the Madison Mart; they are
all important buildings in the city's history.

> *They* is a plural pronoun referring to the antecedents
> *Kingsmore Building, Avondale Tower,* and *Madison*
> *Mart*—which are plural because they are connected by
> *and.*

3.   Two or more singular antecedents joined by *or* or *nor* are referred to by a singular pronoun.

> Either Jack or Tom will be ready when he is called.
>
> > No matter which of the two antecedents *(Jack, Tom)* is se-
> > lected, the result will be a singular masculine anteced-
> > ent; therefore, the pronoun *he* is singular and agrees with
> > the antecedent in number.

Neither Sue nor Marie has advanced in the firm as rapidly as
she expected.

> *She* is the correct singular pronoun choice because the
> two singular antecedents joined by *nor* are both female.

When one of the choices is singular and the other is plural, however, the pronoun should agree with the nearer antecedent. This
situation, of course, is similar to that of singular subjects joined by
or or *nor*, which we discussed under Subject-Verb Agreement.

> Neither the doctor nor the nurses will be well received
> when they announce the decision.
>
> > *Doctor* is singular, and *nurses* is plural; since the
> > plural *nurses* is nearer the pronoun, the plural pro-
> > noun *they* is the correct choice.

On the other hand, if the two antecedents were reversed, the pronoun would have to change.

pl.   sing.

Neither the nurses nor the doctor will be well received

    sing.

when he announces the decision.

4.   Collective nouns will be referred to by either singular or plural pronouns depending on meaning.

The team follows its coach's orders.
The team discuss their differences at every meeting.

Both sentences are correct. In the first, *team* is considered a unit (singular) and is referred to by the singular pronoun *its*. Pronoun and antecedent agree in number. In the second sentence, *team* is considered as separate individual members (plural) and is referred to by the plural pronoun *their*. Pronoun and antecedent agree. Notice in both cases that due to the verb only one pronoun can be correct. As soon as you say *The team follows*, the -*s* on the verb makes *team* singular. To say *The team follows their coach's orders* would be inconsistent and therefore incorrect. Similarly, when you say *The team discuss* you have made the collective noun plural, and it requires a plural pronoun.

5.   The pronoun *who* is usually used in referring to people; the pronoun *which* in referring to animals and things; and the pronoun *that* in referring to either persons, places, animals, or things.

Person: There is the contestant who is most likely to win the pageant.

Animal: The dog that steals Mr. Brown's newspaper is an Irish setter.

Thing: My aunt's hand-carved bed, which she bought last year, is a beautiful piece of furniture.

Place: It is New York that I like most of all.

7

Identifying and Correcting Sentence Fragments

A sentence fragment is part of a sentence. But what is a sentence? Some people consider a sentence to be a word or group of words that expresses a complete thought. This definition, however, brings up another question: "What is a complete thought?" Just as the part of speech of a word in a particular sentence can be determined only by how the word is used in context, what may be considered a complete thought in one context may not make sense in another. For example, if someone you did not know and had not spoken with came up to you and said, "flying," you might think the person was crazy. On the other hand, if you asked someone, "Are you flying or driving to the conference in Chicago?" the one-word answer *flying* would express a complete thought. Similarly, if you ask someone, "Will you go to the dance with me Saturday night?" the one-word answer *yes* or *no* is a complete thought. Clearly, whether an expression is considered a complete thought or not depends on the context.

Some writers, however, unintentionally treat incomplete thoughts as correct sentences. Such "sentences" can be very distracting to readers. Therefore, you should learn what a grammatically complete sentence is in order to avoid unintentional fragments. **A grammatically complete sentence is a word or group of words that contains a subject and verb (either stated or implied) and expresses a complete thought.**

John Victor owns over 1,000 books.

The sentence contains the verb *owns* and the subject *John Victor,* and the statement is a complete thought.

Jump!

The sentence contains the verb *jump*, and it has the implied sub-ject *you*. The sentence is grammatically complete and expresses a complete thought. A sentence fragment, then, is a word or group of words beginning with a capital letter and ending with a period, exclamation point, or question mark that is not grammatically complete or that does not express a complete thought.

And was rowing hard to reach the lighthouse.

The group of words is a fragment. It does not contain a subject, and it does not express a complete thought.

You should strive to make your sentences grammatically complete. Although some writers occasionally construct inten-tional fragments, papers that are written primarily to inform the reader should avoid fragments. In informative writing, your main goal is clarity. Fragments do not help you attain this goal. Most sentence fragments are unintentional and are usually a result of rapid writing and poor proofreading. The first part of this chapter will help you learn to identify sentence fragments; the second part will give you guidance on how to eliminate fragments in your writing.

Types of Sentence Fragments

Knowing the most common types of sentence fragments can help you avoid using them. In general, four types of word groups are mistaken for sentences: (1) phrases, (2) subordinate clauses, (3) nouns followed by modifiers, and (4) sentences beginning with *and* or *but*.

Phrases as Fragments

One of the most common sentence fragment errors is mistaking phrases for grammatically complete sentences. Remember, a phrase is a group of related words that does not contain a subject and verb. Since a phrase contains no subject and verb, it cannot be a grammatically complete sentence. Also, a phrase does not ex-press a complete thought. Even if a prepositional, infinitive, participial, or gerund phrase begins with a capital letter and ends with a period, it is still a fragment.

> In that gigantic swamp in Harlow County.
>> The two prepositional phrases constitute a fragment.

> To do the job adequately and proficiently.
>> The infinitive phrase is a fragment.

> Having eaten thirteen bowls of oyster soup.
>> The participial phrase is a fragment.

> Generating fifty kilowatts per day.
>> The verbal phrase (potentially either participle or gerund) is a fragment.

Proofread your writing to see that you have not carelessly treated a phrase as a complete sentence.

Subordinate Clauses as Fragments

Another type of sentence fragment error is mistaking subordinate clauses for complete sentences. Remember, a subordinate clause is a group of related words that contains a subject and a verb but that does not express a complete thought.

Note: A group of related words that contains a subject and a verb is not necessarily a grammatically complete sentence.

Since a subordinate clause depends on the main clause to complete its meaning, it cannot stand alone as a sentence.

> Until the stadium is cleaned of all debris.
> Whoever is elected to the student government association.
> Which is a fine stream for trout fishing.

All the previous word groups are fragments. You must be careful in your writing to avoid such fragments.

Noun Followed by Modifier as Fragment

Though phrases and subordinate clauses mistakenly treated as complete sentences are the main causes of fragments, there are others. Often a noun will be followed by an adjective clause that modifies it:

> The pilot who shot down the Red Baron in World War I.

Who shot down the Red Baron in World War I is an adjective clause modifying the noun *pilot*. The entire group of words beginning with *The* and ending with the period is a fragment because it does not express a complete thought. The noun *pilot* appears to be a subject, but there is no verb for it to be the subject of. The fragment can be made into a complete sentence simply by supplying a verb:

> The pilot who shot down the Red Baron in World War I was not Eddie Rickenbacker.

Now the noun *pilot* is the subject of the verb *was* and the group of words is a complete sentence.

Fragments Caused by Beginning Sentences with *And* or *But*

Another way writers mistakenly create fragments is by beginning sentences with the word *and* or *but*.

> And was forced to find an alternative procedure.

The group of words is a fragment because there is no subject for the verb *was forced*. Because the mistake with *and* is so easy to commit, many teachers tell students not to begin sentences with the words *and* or *but*. Actually, there is nothing grammatically wrong with beginning a sentence with the words *and* or *but* as long as what follows is a grammatically complete sentence. If the preceding sentence had been written *And the astronaut was forced to find an alternative procedure,* the sentence would have been grammatically complete. In fact, words like *and* and *but* can sometimes be effective in making sentences flow together smoothly.

Bob wants to ask Carol Downs to the class picnic. But he is afraid to ask her.

By setting the second sentence off with a period and a capital letter, the writer has emphasized Bob's lack of courage. Of course, such sentences beginning with coordinate conjunctions are generally used for either transition or emphasis; therefore, as with most effective writing techniques, they should be used sparingly. It is important to be sure that sentences beginning with coordinate conjunctions are grammatically complete.

Correcting Sentence Fragments

Now that you have an understanding of sentence fragments, you should be able to proofread your own papers and remove any fragments you may have accidentally written. The two main things to check for in proofreading are (1) that each group of words treated as a sentence does contain a subject and a verb and (2) that each group of words treated as a sentence containing a subject and a verb does not begin with either a subordinate conjunction or a relative pronoun. If the group of words does not contain a subject and a verb, it is probably a phrase. If the word group contains a subject and a verb but is introduced by a relative pronoun or a subordinate conjunction, it is probably a subordinate clause.

In the event your proofreading does turn up a sentence fragment, you should not have much trouble correcting the error. Fragments can be corrected in several ways. One of the easiest ways is to attach the fragment to another sentence.

Fragment: I really like to go swimming. In the pond near Ms. Johnson's apiary.

Correct the fragment by attaching it to the complete sentence:

Full Sentence: I really like to go swimming in the pond near Ms. Johnson's apiary.

Fragment: After I finished the novel. I went to bed.

Correct the fragment by attaching it to the complete sentence:

Full Sentence: After I finished the novel, I went to bed.

Fragments can also be corrected by supplying the missing subjects or verbs.

Fragment: The antique that I purchased in Williamsburg, Virginia.

Correct the fragment by providing the noun *antique* with a verb:

Full Sentence: The antique that I purchased in Williamsburg, Virginia, disintegrated.

Now *antique* is the subject of the verb *disintegrated* and the sentence is complete.

Fragment: But was not completed by the July 15 deadline.

Correct the fragment by providing the verb *was completed* with a subject:

Full Sentence: But the project was not completed by the July 15 deadline.

Now *project* is the subject of the verb *was completed* and the sentence is complete.

Occasionally a fragment is so fragmentary or so confused that it must be completely rewritten.

Fragment: The botanical gardens in Chapel Hill, North Carolina, being the place.

The group of words should be completely rewritten:

Full Sentence: Only plants native to North Carolina can be found in the botanical gardens in Chapel Hill, North Carolina.

Be sure not to confuse verbals and verbs. The *-ing* form of a verb cannot be a main verb without an auxiliary.

Fragment: The bridge being over two thousand feet long.

Being is a verbal, not a verb. The verbal should be converted into a main verb.

Full Sentence: The bridge *is* over two thousand feet long.

8

Identifying and Correcting Fused Sentences and Comma Splices

When studying comma splices and fused sentences, you are learning as much about punctuation as you are about grammar. In this chapter, you will first learn to recognize these types of sentence errors; then you will see the four ways in which fused or comma-spliced sentences can be corrected.

Fused Sentences

A *fused sentence* is the result of combining main clauses without putting any punctuation between them.

> I saw Shakespeare's *Henry IV, Part One*, last night this evening I am going to see *Henry IV, Part Two*.

The break between main clauses is between the words *night* and *this*. Because no punctuation is present, the sentence is fused.

> I saw *Henry IV, Part One*, last night this evening I am going to see *Henry IV, Part Two*, next week I will attend *Henry V* I look forward to seeing every play.

Now the sentence is fused in three places—between *night* and *this*, between *Two* and *next*, between *V* and *I*.

There are two correct ways to join the main clauses of a compound sentence: use (1) a semicolon or (2) a comma and one of the coordinate conjunctions *(and, or, nor, but, yet, so)*.

John Davis spent over thirty hours preparing the report for his boss; it was never read.

> The sentence is correct because a semicolon joins the break between the main clauses.

John Davis spent over thirty hours preparing the report for his boss, but it was never read.

> The sentence is correct because the comma and the coordinate conjunction *but* join the break between main clauses.

Notice that the sentence with the semicolon packs a punch. It is more direct and forceful. Although the sentence with the comma and the coordinating conjunction gives the same information, the fact that John Davis' report was not read has been de-emphasized by the inclusion of the comma and coordinating conjunction. Thus, in your writing the punctuation you use can determine the emphasis you wish to place on an idea. Naturally, the main clauses being joined must be logically related.

> I bought a Panasonic radio, and *Ulysses* was banned in this country until 1933.

Though the sentence is correctly punctuated, it is an extremely bad sentence. No amount of punctuation can improve such an illogical sentence.

Comma Splices

Now that you know how the main clauses of a sentence can be correctly joined by a comma, look at how they are often incorrectly joined by a comma. The *comma splice* error is the result of combining main clauses with a comma where the comma is insufficient punctuation.

> Mary is a dedicated homemaker on the weekends, she vacuums the floors and puts everything in its proper place.
>
> The break between main clauses occurs between *weekends* and *she*. The sentence is comma spliced since a comma is not sufficient punctuation to join the main clauses.

Mary is a dedicated homemaker on the weekends, she vac-
uums the floors and puts everything in its proper place,
then on Monday she ignores the house, she will not per-
form any domestic chores until Friday.

Now the sentence is comma spliced three times: between *weekends* and *she,* between *place* and *then,* and
between *house* and *she.* Remember, a sentence that is
comma spliced always contains a comma.

Conjunctive Adverbs and Transitional Phrases

Words such as *however* and expressions such as *on the other hand*
often occur at the break between main clauses. Such words and
expressions are modifiers that are used to connect clauses. The
individual words are called *conjunctive adverbs;* the multiword
expressions are called *transitional phrases.* Conjunctive adverbs
and transitional phrases are not coordinate conjunctions and cannot connect main clauses with just a comma.

My professor likes the novelist John Gardner, however, she
believes John Updike is a better craftsman.

The sentence is comma spliced between *Gardner* and
however. To keep the sentence compound, you would
need to use a semicolon.

My professor likes the novelist John Gardner; however, she
believes John Updike is a better craftsman.

Many of the following words and phrases appear at the break between main clauses.

Conjunctive Adverbs	*Transitional Phrases*
accordingly	as a result
also	at the same time
besides	for example
consequently	in addition
furthermore	in fact

Conjunctive Adverbs	Transitional Phrases
hence	in other words
henceforth	on the contrary
however	on the other hand
indeed	that is
likewise	
meanwhile	
moreover	
nevertheless	
otherwise	
still	
then	
therefore	
thus	

It may be easier to understand the difference between pure co-ordinate conjunctions and the words and phrases on the list above if you realize that conjunctions are used to connect, whereas the listed words and phrases help the sentence flow smoothly.

In the following sentence, *but* can be only where it is; it does not fit or make sense in any other position:

Correct: Ralph likes his secretary a great deal, but he likes his wife even more.

Incorrect: Ralph likes his secretary a great deal; he but likes his wife even more.

. **Incorrect:** Ralph likes his secretary a great deal; he likes his wife even more but.

Notice that versions 2 and 3 are awkward and nonsensical. The reason is that *but* is a pure conjunction and can only be used to connect.

On the other hand, a word such as *however* can fit in several positions in the sentence and still make sense:

Ralph likes his secretary a great deal; however, he likes his wife even more.

1. Ralph likes his secretary a great deal; he likes his wife, however, even more.

2. Ralph likes his secretary a great deal; he likes his wife even more, however.

The word *however* (and the other words and phrases listed) can be moved around in the sentence because it is not a pure connector.

Remember, only coordinate conjunctions can connect main clauses with just a comma before them; the other words and phrases cannot. Avoid sentences such as the following:

> Jane thought she wanted to go to dental school she decided, however, to major in drama instead.
> > Though the sentence contains the word *however* with a comma before it, the sentence is fused between *school* and *she* and not comma spliced, since *however* is not at the break between clauses.

Most important, you should remember that a sentence can be neither comma spliced nor fused if it does not contain at least two main clauses.

> *Short Fiction of the Masters* is a good anthology.
> > The sentence is just a simple sentence containing one main clause.

Ways to Correct Comma Splices and Fused Sentences

There are four ways to correct comma splices and fused sentences.

> **Fused:** Jane thought she wanted to go to dental school she decided to major in drama instead.

> **Comma splice:** Jane thought she wanted to go to dental school, she decided to major in drama instead.

1.   The main clauses can be rewritten as separate sentences:

Jane thought she wanted to go to dental school. She decided to major in drama instead.

2.   One of the main clauses can be rewritten as a subordinate clause:

Although Jane thought she wanted to go to dental school, she decided to major in drama instead.

3.   A semicolon can be put between the main clauses:

Jane thought she wanted to go to dental school; she decided to major in drama instead.

4.   A comma and a coordinate conjunction can be put at the break between clauses:

Jane thought she wanted to go to dental school, but she decided to major in drama instead.

The way you choose to correct a comma splice will depend on your personal preferences and on the meaning you wish to convey. For example, the coordinate conjunction *and* balances two main clauses, whereas the coordinate conjunctions *but* and *yet* contrast them.

Balancing: Robert wanted to buy Janice an expensive winter coat, and he went to the nicest store in town to find one.

Contrasting: Robert wanted to buy Janice an expensive winter coat, but he could not afford to get the one he really liked.

Subordinating one of the clauses de-emphasizes it.

De-emphasizing: Although Robert wanted to buy Janice an expensive winter coat, he couldn't afford to get the one he really liked.

Combining two main clauses in one sentence with a semi-colon between them gives each clause equal emphasis and indicates the close relationship in meaning between the two.

Equalizing: Robert wanted to buy Janice an expensive winter coat; he went to the nicest store in town to find one.

Putting the main clauses in two separate sentences emphasizes each one more.

Emphasizing: Robert wanted to buy Janice an expensive winter coat. He could not afford to get the one he really liked.

No one method of correcting comma splices and fused sentences is more correct than another. Just strive for variety in your writing and avoid overworking any one technique.

9

Pronoun Case and Reference

Case

Pronouns are naming words that are used to take the place of nouns. Just like nouns, pronouns usually function as subjects, direct objects, indirect objects, objects of prepositions, and predicate nominatives. The case of a pronoun shows its function in a sentence. There are three cases in English: nominative, objective, and possessive. Here is a list of pronouns classified by case:

Nominative	Objective	Possessive
I	me	my (mine)
you	you	your (yours)
it	it	its
we	us	our (ours)
he, she	him, her	his, her (hers)
they	them	their (theirs)
who	whom	whose
whoever	whomever	

Nominative Case

1. Pronouns used as subjects require the nominative case.

I am going to get a loan today.
> *I* is in the nominative case because it is the subject of the verb *am going*.

They will complete the float in time for the parade.
They is in the nominative case because it is the subject of the verb *will complete.*

2. Pronouns used as predicate nominatives require the nominative case.

The winner was he who spoke first.
He is in the nominative case because it is a predicate nominative.

It is I.
I functions as a predicate nominative and is therefore in the nominative case.

3. An appositive is a noun or pronoun that renames or explains another noun or pronoun. When an appositive renames a word in the nominative case, it too is in the nominative case.

Two men, John and Bob, attended the special dinner.
Men is the subject of the verb *attended* and is therefore in the nominative case. The words *John* and *Bob* rename the noun *men* and are therefore appositives.

Two men, Bob and I, attended the special dinner.
Now *I* is a pronoun in the nominative case. It is in apposition with the subject *men*, which is a noun in the nominative case.

The girls, Judy and she, built a model of the Globe Theatre.
She is in the nominative case because it is in apposition with a word in the nominative case, the subject *girls.*

Objective Case

1. Pronouns used as objects require the objective case. The most common types of objects are direct objects, indirect objects, and objects of prepositions.

Do you really love her?
Her is in the objective case because it is the direct object of the verb *do love.*

Judy gave him a sweater for his birthday.
> *Him* is in the objective case because it is the indirect
> object of the verb *gave*.

Give the free pass to me.
> *Me* is in the objective case because it is the object of
> the preposition *to*.

2.   The objective case is also used for a pronoun that functions as
the object of a verbal.
To arrest him is the FBI's goal.
> *Him* is in the objective case because it is the object of the
> infinitive *to arrest*.

Getting him to the podium at last, Judy sat down.
> *Him* is in the objective case because it is the object of the
> participle *getting*.

3.   And a pronoun in apposition with a word in the objective case
goes in the objective case.

The committee elected two representatives—Susan and me.
> *Me* is in the objective case because it is in apposition
> with the direct object *representatives*.

Save the biggest applause for the finalists—the Cardinals
and us.
> *Us* is in apposition with the word *finalists*, which is the
> object of the preposition *for*.

Remember that a pronoun appositive can be in either the objective or nominative case, depending on the case of the word the
pronoun is in apposition with. You should also realize that the
pronoun itself may take an appositive.

We runners were breathing hard during the race.
> *Runners* is in apposition with the pronoun *we*. *We* is
> used correctly in the nominative case because it is the
> subject of the verb *were breathing*.

The coach gave the trophy to us winners.
> *Us* is used correctly in the objective case because it is

the object of the preposition *to*. *Winners* is an appositive and does not affect the pronoun choice.

Who / Whom

You need to be careful when *who* and *whom* appear in subordinate clauses. *Who* and *whoever* are nominative case forms that
will ordinarily function as subjects. But *who* and *whoever* will
often be the subjects of the subordinate clauses in which they appear, not necessarily the subject of the whole sentence.

Who will win the British Open this year?
    In this sentence *who* is the subject of the whole sen-
    tence since *will win* is the only verb.

Whoever picks the most cucumbers will win a bushel of corn.
    In this sentence *whoever* is the subject of the verb
    picks, but the whole noun clause *whoever picks the
    most cucumbers* is the subject of the whole sentence.
    Whoever is just the subject of the verb in its clause.

John likes whoever travels to the games with him.
    Whoever is the subject of the verb *travels*. The whole
    noun clause *whoever travels to the games with him* is
    the direct object of the verb *likes*.

A subordinate who/whom clause may function as an object of
a preposition.

He worked with whoever needed him most.
    Whoever needed him most is the object of the preposi-
    tion *with*. *Whoever* is the subject of the verb *needed* in
    the subordinate clause.

The subordinate who/whom clauses may have other functions.

Knowing (who, whom) would win the election, the mayor
withdrew from the race.
    Who is the subject of the verb *would win*. The whole
    noun clause *who would win the election* is the object
    of the participle *knowing*.

Give (whoever, whomever) eats the most an Alka-Seltzer tablet.

> *Whoever* is the subject of the verb *eats*. The whole noun clause *whoever eats the most* is an indirect object of the verb *give*.

Arthur Hall is a man (who, whom) greatly admires the films of W. C. Fields.

> This time the subordinate clause is an adjective clause. *Who greatly admires the films of W. C. Fields* modifies the noun *man*. *Who* is the correct choice because it is the subject of the verb *admires*.

When the verb in a subordinate who/whom clause already has a subject, the correct choice is usually *whom*, functioning as a direct object of the verb in the subordinate clause.

Whomever she prefers will be appointed.

Whomever she prefers is the noun clause subject of the verb *will be appointed*. Within the noun clause *she* is the subject of the verb *prefers*; she prefers whom? the answer is *whomever*. Once you realize that the verb *prefers* already has a subject, you should realize that *whomever* is the direct object.

The woman (who, whom) John loves is a truck driver.

> *Whom* is the correct choice because it is the direct object of the verb *loves* in the subordinate clause.

You should be careful with who/whom clauses in sentences that contain expressions such as *I think, I feel, I believe, you may recall*, etc. Such expressions are merely parenthetical interrupters that are not grammatically relevant. The expressions have to be mentally ignored.

Janet is the girl who I think deserves the award.

> *Janet* is the subject of the verb *is*, and *who* is the subject of the verb *deserves*.

If you are careful in your writing to make sure each verb has a subject, you will avoid sentences such as *Janet is the girl whom I think deserves the award*. If *whom* were considered the object of the verb *think*, the verb *deserves* would not have a subject.

Pronouns are sometimes used following such words as *than* and *as*. Often such uses only imply a subject and/or verb. You must recognize what is omitted.

Fred likes Kathy better than I.
Fred likes Kathy better than me.

Both sentences are correct, but they mean quite different things. The first sentence has an implied verb:

Fred likes Kathy better than I [do].
I is the subject of the understood verb *do* (or *like*).

The second has an implied subject and verb.

Fred likes Kathy better than [he likes] me.
Me is the object of the understood expression *he* likes.

In your own writing you want to communicate the right message to the reader. The sentence ending with *I* means something very different indeed from the one ending with *me*. As Mark Twain said, "The difference between the right word and the almost right word is the difference between lightning and the lightning bug."

Possessive Case

The possessive case is generally used before a gerund.

Mr. Jones does not like Susan's staying out past midnight.
The proper noun *Susan* is possessive because it precedes the gerund *staying*.

His practicing four hours each day won him the prize.
His is in the possessive case. It precedes the gerund *practicing*, which is the subject of the verb *won*.

He soon tired of our complaining.
Our is in the possessive case because it precedes the gerund *complaining*, the object of the preposition *of*.

Reference

As a writer you need to be certain your pronouns are in the right case. You must also be sure the noun the pronoun stands for (the antecedent) is obvious to the reader. When the reader cannot tell what noun the pronoun refers to, the writer has put up a barrier to communication known as faulty pronoun reference. There is more than one type of faulty pronoun reference to avoid.

1. Avoid sentences that have two possible antecedents for a pronoun.

> **Incorrect:** Susan told Jane that she had an attractive coiffure.

The pronoun is *she*, but is the antecedent *Susan* or *Jane?*

> **Correct:** Susan told Jane, "You have an attractive coiffure."

Now the reader knows that Jane has the attractive coiffure.

> **Incorrect:** Bob told Ralph that he had stolen three dollars.

Is the antecedent of *he* supposed to be *Bob* or *Ralph?*

> **Correct:** Bob confessed to Ralph that he had stolen three dollars.

Now the reader knows that the antecedent of *he* is *Bob*.

2. Avoid sentences that have antecedents remote from the pronoun. An antecedent is said to be remote if it is too far from the pronoun.

> The noise was disturbing to everyone in the class. The teacher felt the rusty machine was to blame. It reached a level of 180 decibels.

Does *it* refer to *noise* or *machine?*

> The noise, which reached a level of 180 decibels, was disturbing to everyone in the class. The teacher felt the rusty machine was to blame.

Now there is no remote pronoun reference. The unclear *it* has been removed.

> The amateur radio operators installed their equipment in the shopping center. The shoppers were very interested. They stayed through the lunch hour.

Does the *they* mean the operators or the shoppers?

> The amateur radio operators installed their equipment in the shopping center; they stayed through the lunch hour. The shoppers were very interested.

Since the pronoun *they* comes in the same sentence as its antecedent *operators* and before the word *shoppers*, the reference is no longer remote.

A special type of obscure reference occurs when the antecedent is in the possessive case.

> While John's car was being repaired, he played nine holes of golf.

The antecedent of *he* is *John's*. Good writers avoid placing the antecedent in the possessive case. One reason is *John's* is an adjective modifying car, telling which car. The antecedent of a pronoun should not be an adjective.

> While John was having his car repaired, he played nine holes of golf.

Now the antecedent of both *his* and *he* is the nonpossessive word *John*.

3. Avoid sentences that have *this, that*, or *which* referring to the general idea of a preceding clause or sentence. Though some writers allow *this, that*, or *which* to refer to general ideas, more precise writers employ a particular word as the antecedent of *this, that*, or *which*.

> **Careless:** Democrats should support the party's candidates. This is what party members are told.

> **Precise:** Party members are told to support the Democratic candidates.

Careless: Everyone wanted the man to stand up for his rights. That is what they came to see.

What is the antecedent of *that?*

Precise: Everyone came to see the man stand up for his rights.

4. Avoid implied antecedents. Antecedents should be stated rather than merely implied.

Implied: Although the test was easy, they had a lot of trouble.

Stated: Although the test was easy, the students had a lot of trouble.

Implied: Joseph Gluck delivered a good sermon. They told him so as they left the church.

Stated: Joseph Gluck delivered a good sermon. The members of the congregation told him so as they left the church.

5. Avoid awkward use of the indefinite *it, you,* or *they.* The awkwardness results from the pronoun's lack of a specific antecedent.

Awkward: It says to jog three miles every day.

Improved: The article says to jog three miles every day.

Awkward: Many states require you to burn the headlight day or night when riding a motorcycle.

Improved: Many states require motorcyclists to burn the headlight day or night.

Awkward: At one revival they said watching television was a sin.

Improved: At one revival the preacher said watching television was a sin.

6. Avoid using both the definite and the indefinite *it* in a sentence.

> **Awkward:** Although it is a good day to clean the pool, it is not extremely dirty.
>> The first *it* is indefinite; the second *it* refers to the noun *pool*.

> **Improved:** Although it is a good day for cleaning, the pool is not extremely dirty.

> **Awkward:** We intended to plant a peach tree this fall. It is too late to plant it now.
>> The first *it* is indefinite; the second *it* refers to the noun *tree*.

> **Improved:** We intended to plant a peach tree this fall. It is too late now.

10

Adjectives and Adverbs

Adjectives and adverbs are modifiers. Adjectives modify nouns and pronouns, and they answer the questions Which one? What kind? and How many? Adverbs modify verbs, adjectives, and other adverbs, and they answer the questions How? When? Why? Where? To what extent? and On what condition?

Forming Adjectives and Adverbs

Some adjectives are formed by adding the endings *-al, -able, -ful, -ish, -ive, -less,* and *-y* to the noun or verb form.

Noun or Verb	Adjective
mayor	mayoral
credit	creditable
fruit	fruitful
self	selfish
progress	progressive
use	useless
sleep	sleepy

Many adverbs are formed by adding the ending *-ly* to adjectives.

Adjective	Adverb
brave	bravely
courageous	courageously
careful	carefully
religious	religiously

However, not all words ending in -*ly* are adverbs. The adjective
lonely is a good example of this. Furthermore, not all adverbs end
in -*ly;* for instance, *very, soon, now,* and *not* are all frequently used
adverbs. Though most words ending in -*ly* function as adverbs, the
only sure way to tell is to see how the word is used in the sentence.
If the word modifies a noun or a pronoun, it is an adjective. If
the word modifies a verb, an adjective, or another adverb, it is an
adverb.

Using Adjectives and Adverbs Correctly

Some writers use adjectives where they should use adverbs and
vice versa. Though such usage is not often a serious barrier to
communication, it can distract the reader. A useful rule to remember is that adverbs generally follow action verbs and adjectives generally follow linking verbs.

> J.P. Wright dances gracefully to any kind of music.
>> The action verb *dances* takes the adverb *gracefully.*
>> *Gracefully* modifies the verb *dances* and answers the
>> question Dances how?

> Mario Andretti drives all racing cars expertly.
>> *Expertly* is an adverb modifying the verb *drives* and an-
>> swers the question Drives how?

> The coffee tastes bitter.
>> The adjective *bitter* follows the linking verb *tastes.*

> The flowers smell sweet.
>> The adjective *sweet* follows the linking verb *smell.*

Linking verbs, which generally take adjectives, do not express
any action; they express a state of existence, being, or emotion.
The adjective following a linking verb usually modifies the
subject.

> Pat Johnson is lazy.
>> *Lazy* is an adjective modifying the subject *Pat Johnson.*
>> *Lazy* is a predicate adjective.

A list of commonly used linking verbs includes:

is		appear
am		become
was	forms of the	seem
were	verb *to be*	taste
been		feel
being		smell
		look
		sound

In your writing, you must be aware of whether the verb is an action verb or a linking verb. Some of the linking verbs in our list can also be action verbs, depending on how they are used in the sentence.

The bottle selling for $1,250 looks fragile.
> *Looks* is a linking verb. The bottle has no eyes with which to look; it is not looking. Therefore, the adjective *fragile* is used to modify the subject *bottle*.

Dick Allen looks carefully at every item on sale.
> In this sentence *looks* is an action verb. Dick Allen has eyes, and he is looking. Therefore, the adverb *carefully* is used to modify the verb *looks*.

Look at these two sentences:

The unblended Scotch tastes bitter.
The man tastes the rare Scotch admiringly.

In the first sentence, the Scotch has no tongue with which to taste, so *tastes* is a linking verb. The subject *Scotch* is modified by the predicate adjective *bitter*. In the second sentence, the man can taste and is doing so. Therefore, the adverb *admiringly* modifies the action verb *tastes*. Do not carelessly use an adjective where an adverb should be used.

Faulty: Sing the song forceful.
Correct: Sing the song forcefully.
> *Forcefully* is an adverb modifying the action verb *sing*.

Faulty: The carpenter is a real fine man.
Correct: The carpenter is a really fine man.
> *Really* is an adverb modifying the adjective *fine*.

Faulty: Jane sure won that event.
Correct: Jane surely won that event.
   Surely is an adverb modifying the verb *won*.

Faulty: John plays his position good.
Correct: John plays his position well.
   Well is an adverb modifying the verb *plays*.

Degrees of Adjectives and Adverbs

Adjectives and adverbs are said to have degrees. The positive degree does not compare; the comparative degree compares two persons or things; and the superlative degree compares three or more persons or things.

Positive degree: Inez is tall.
Comparative degree: Sharon is taller than Carletta.
Superlative degree: Mary is the tallest girl in the dorm.

Look at the following chart:

Number of Syllables in Word	Positive Degree	Comparative Degree	Superlative Degree
1	rich	richer	richest
1	brave	braver	bravest
2	fancy	fancier	fanciest
2	handsome	more handsome	most handsome
3	beautiful	more beautiful	most beautiful
4	mysterious	more mysterious	most mysterious

Notice that adjectives of one syllable form the comparative degree by adding *-er* to the positive degree and form the superlative degree by adding *-est* to the positive degree. (*Brave, braver, bravest* is an exception only because the *e* is already on the word.) Notice that adjectives of three syllables or more form the comparative degree by adding the word *more* before the positive degree and the superlative degree by adding the word *most*. The words *more* and *most* in the comparative and superlative degrees indicate an ascending comparison.

> Bob is more intelligent than Ralph.
> Albert is the most intelligent of all.

To indicate a descending comparison, use the words *less* and *least*:

> Bob is less intelligent than Ralph.
> Albert is the least intelligent of all.

The chart indicates that words of two syllables may use either the *-er, -est* forms or the *more, most* forms. The main thing to remember, however, is that the two different forms should never be mixed. If you use *-er*, do not use *more*. It is poor usage to say *Bob is more richer than Ralph.*

Some comparative forms are irregular. These irregular forms must be memorized.

Positive	Comparative	Superlative
bad, badly	worse	worst
far	farther, further	farthest, furthest
good, well	better	best
little	less	least
many, much	more	most
several, some		

Make sure your comparisons are logical. Some words are absolute in meaning and cannot be compared. *Unique, empty, dead, perfect, entirely, round* are all absolutes. If a snowflake is unique, it is unique. It makes no sense to say one snowflake is more unique than another. The word *unique* means *one of a kind*, and thus by definition the word allows no comparison.

Using Nouns as Modifiers

Some writers awkwardly use nouns as adjectives. In a sentence such as *Marlene Draughn is interested in theater history*, the noun *theater* is used as an adjective modifying *history.* The sentence is effective. However, in a sentence like *Jack Nelson is a mayor candidate,* the use of the noun *mayor* as an adjective modifying *candidate* is ineffective. The correct word is the adjective *mayoral,* a mayoral candidate.

PUNCTUATION AND MECHANICS

11

Commas

The comma is a punctuation mark that separates, introduces, and shows omission.

Though a comma indicates only a brief pause, its presence or absence can have a strong effect on the clarity of a sentence. If a writer fails to put a comma in where it is needed, the reader might misinterpret the sentence.

> The government supplied guns, tanks, bulletproof cars and trucks.
>
> Were the trucks also bulletproof? They would seem to be, judging by the punctuation.

As always, though, language and punctuation are changing. The trend in recent years has been, "when in doubt, don't." In other words, if you cannot think of a specific reason why the comma should be used, leave it out. In this chapter we will explain the specific instances where commas should be used. In order to help you group the numerous rules under a few general headings, the uses of the comma have been subdivided as follows:

Main clauses
Introductory elements
Items in a series and coordinate adjectives
Nonrestrictive, parenthetical, and contrasting elements
Dates, degrees, place names, and long numbers
Unnecessary commas

Main Clauses

Use commas to separate main clauses when they are joined by *and, or, nor, but, yet,* and *so.*

> I find the study of the English language interesting, but I do not understand the confusing spelling rules.

> Mr. James Fincaster is a lawyer in New York City, and his son is an accountant there.

Note: Some writers do not use a comma before a coordinate conjunction connecting two short main clauses, especially if the subject is the same in both clauses.

> Mary washed her hair and then she blow-dried it.

Introductory Elements

1.   Use commas to set off long (one-half line or more) introductory adverb clauses.

> Although the weather was ideal, Jane wouldn't leave the house.

> If the aldermen would only act, the problem would be resolved.

Notice that adverb clauses tacked on to the end of a sentence do not have to be set off with commas:

> Jane wouldn't leave the house although the weather was ideal.

2.   Use commas to set off introductory verbal phrases.

> Plying his trade expertly, the salesman sold the woman a car she couldn't afford.

> To be perfectly honest, Gerald Smitherman cannot handle that job.

3. Use commas to set off long (one-half line or more) introductory prepositional phrases.

> In the dugout after the second game of a doubleheader, the catcher looked as if he couldn't even stand up.

> After eating three sixteen-inch pizzas in twenty minutes, Bob was still hungry.

4. Use commas to set off absolute constructions that come at the beginning of a sentence. **An absolute construction is a word or group of words that relates to the thought of the sentence in which it is found, but is not grammatically related to any particular word in the sentence.**

> **Adverb absolute:**   Interestingly enough, no one had any desire to lead the new club.

> **Nominative absolute:**   The gate not yet being open to the public, Dale and Yvonne had to park three blocks away.

5. Use commas to set off nouns of direct address.

> John, did you go to the Kiwanis Club meeting last night?

> Barbara, please pick me up two king-size sheets if they are on sale.

6. Use commas to set off mild interjections and *yes* or *no* answers followed by more explanation.

> Well, I guess I could have done a better job if I had prepared more thoroughly.

> Yes, I believe Bob does intend to go to the district meeting.

7. Use commas to set off introductory conjunctive adverbs and transitional phrases. (See pages 87–88.)

> Nevertheless, Jane is still the best person for the job even though she does work slowly.

> On the other hand, the commissioners could just rezone the whole area.

8.   Use commas to introduce short quotations.

Mary said, "Nellie Forbush has to wash her hair in every performance of *South Pacific*."

The young quarterback whispered to the coach, "Some of the starters broke the team rules last night."

9.   Use commas to set off some introductory expressions in order to prevent misreading.

A few days before Bob set out on a trip and wrecked his car.
   The sentence needs a comma after *before* to prevent misreading.

A few days before, Bob set out on a trip and wrecked his car.

In 1979 273 people were killed in a DC-10 crash.
   The sentence needs a comma between the numbers.

In 1979, 273 people were killed in a DC-10 crash.
   Better yet, rewrite it.

The crash of a DC-10 in 1979 killed 273 people.

Items in a Series and Coordinate Adjectives

1.   Use commas to separate words, phrases, and clauses in a series.

I like apples, oranges, bananas, and pears.
   Use the comma before the *and* unless the last two items go together: Jim's favorite entertainers are the Bravos, James Pawn, and Donna Gilbert and the Tonsils.

The driver lost control of his car and drove it over the guardrail, through the crowd, and down the embankment.

You need to watch your budget when you are constantly in debt, when you have to borrow to cover routine expenses, and when you feel compelled to buy clothes you don't need.

Go to the bookstore, buy an interesting-looking best-seller, and read it over the weekend.

2. Use a comma to separate coordinate adjectives. (Coordinate adjectives are equal adjectives that modify the same noun.)

A college student receives a meaningful, versatile education that will provide a broader view of life than could be obtained by on-the-job training.

Walden is an interesting, thought-provoking book.

Note: Many adjectives that refer to the number, age (old, young, new), origin, size, color, or location of the noun are so closely related to the nouns they modify that commas are not necessary. A useful rule of thumb is that if the word *and* can replace the comma without creating an awkward effect, then the comma is appropriate.

Sandra is a beautiful American girl.
The sentence would be awkward if it read *Sandra is a beautiful and American girl;* therefore, it would be equally awkward with a comma: *Sandra is a beautiful, American girl.*

There were many satisfied senior citizens when the Social Security increase came into effect.
The sentence would be awkward indeed if it read, *There were many and satisfied and senior citizens when the Social Security increase came into effect.* Similarly, commas would only be distracting: *There were many, satisfied, senior citizens when the Social Security increase came into effect.*

Nonessential, Parenthetical, and Contrasting Elements

1. Use commas to set off nonessential adjective clauses and phrases. A nonessential (or nonrestrictive) clause or phrase is one that is not necessary to *identify* the noun it modifies.

Karen and Pam, with their bathing suits on and their suit-cases in the trunk, headed for the beach.

> The phrase *with their bathing suits on and their suit-cases in the trunk* is not necessary to identify the nouns *Karen* and *Pam*.

Mr. Thomas Atkins appears to be very rich, always wearing cashmere topcoats and Brooks Brothers' suits.

> *Always wearing cashmere topcoats and Brooks Brothers' suits* is a nonessential participial phrase placed at the end of the sentence. The phrase is not necessary to identify Mr. Atkins.

The Carthage High School cheerleaders, who were dressed in their cheerleading uniforms, had to be at the stadium an hour before game time.

> The clause *who were dressed in their cheerleading uniforms* is not necessary to identify the noun *cheerleaders*.

Note that essential (or restrictive) adjective clauses and phrases are *not* set off by commas.

The workers participating in the walkout were fired.

> The phrase *participating in the walkout* is necessary to identify the noun *workers*. All workers were not fired, only those participating in the walkout. The phrase restricts the meaning of the sentence.

Students who cheat on tests are not respected by their teachers.

> Teachers do respect most of their students. It is the ones who cheat that are not respected. Thus, the clause *who cheat on tests* is essential and should not be set off with commas.

Adjective clauses beginning with the word *that* are essential.

Daisy Miller bought a novel that was written by Henry James.

Most adjective clauses following proper names are nonessential.

Susan B. Anthony, who was outspoken on the issue of women's rights, is now honored on a dollar coin.

Most adjective clauses following references to one's parents are nonessential.

> My mother, who is a fine woman, lives in Portland, Maine.

Sometimes adjective clauses and phrases can be either essential or nonessential depending on what is meant.

> The truck driver is very concerned about the Arabian horses, which were killed in the wreck.
>> With the comma the sentence indicates that all of the Arabian horses were killed.

> The truck driver is very concerned about the Arabian horses which were killed in the wreck.
>> Without the comma the sentence indicates that only some of the Arabian horses were killed.

2. Use commas to set off nonessential appositives.

> The owner, a self-made man, would not pay any player more than $250,000 a year.

> She photographed Mount St. Helens, the only active volcano in the continental United States.

Most one-word appositives are not set off with commas.

> My son Tommy is a fast learner.
> Roy Rogers' horse Trigger is stuffed.

3. Nonessential titles are set off with commas. Essential titles are not set off.

> Some Hemingway short stories, such as "The Killers" and "The Short Happy Life of Francis Macomber," are often anthologized.
>> The phrase containing the titles is not essential to the meaning of the sentence.

> The Yeats poem "Sailing to Byzantium" is one of the finest poems of the twentieth century.
>> The title is essential to the meaning of the sentence; without it the reader would not know which poem by Yeats was meant.

4.   Use commas to set off parenthetical elements. (A parenthetical element is any word or expression that abruptly interrupts the flow of a sentence.) Parenthetical elements are not always introducers.

> The project, of course, needs more study.
> James Rein was unable to finish the book by the deadline, however.

Most writers use commas to set off the longer conjunctive adverbs such as *however, moreover, furthermore, consequently*, and *nevertheless*. The shorter ones such as *also, too, still, then*, and *thus* are not always set off.

> Thus the exercise was never actually completed.

5.   Use commas with direct quotations to set off expressions such as *he said, she replied*, and *I shouted*.

> "The lens is made in Germany," the photographer said, "and it should be just what you need."

6.   Use commas to set off contrasted elements.

> Give the job to Ensign Davis, not Sergeant Parker.
> Margaret could give up cigarettes, but not fattening foods.

Dates, Degrees, Place Names, and Long Numbers

1.   Use commas to set off the items in a date.

> On January 5, 1989, Leroy Holrod celebrated his eighty-fourth birthday.

Note: Commas are optional when only the month and year are given.

> In May 1988 Nelson Swaim received his D.Ed. degree.

2. Use commas to set off titles and degrees after proper names.

N. P. Acumen, C.P.A.
Dr. Sharon Everett, Dean of Financial Services
Mr. Carl Brim, Chairperson

3. Use commas to set off geographical locations.

South Bend, Indiana, is the home of Notre Dame.

My mother lives at 2102 Seacrest Lane, Duluth, Minnesota.

4. Use commas after every group of three digits, counting from the right in figures of one thousand or more.

2,394
9,643,298
$259,128

Unnecessary Commas

Now that you have studied the basic comma rules, you should feel more confident about when to use commas. At this point, however, a reminder of where not to use commas may be helpful. A comma indicates a pause, but not every pause needs a comma. In fact, there are certain brief pauses that should not have commas. In the following examples, the circled commas are unnecessary.

1. Except when there are intervening elements, do not use a comma to separate a subject from its verb.

The blind man with the white cane ⊙ walks downtown and back every Sunday.

2. Do not use a comma to separate a verb from its object.

Betty Ann honestly believed ⊙ that she could defeat her boyfriend in a wrestling match.

3. Do not unnecessarily use a comma before a coordinate conjunction.

Jennifer is both an excellent golfer ⊙ and a fine tennis player.

4.   Do not use a comma to set off most introductory words or short phrases.

In 1964 ⊙ Muriel Thomas graduated from Mount Park High School.

Today ⊙ forty men completed their annual two weeks of training camp.

5.   Do not use commas to set off restrictive phrases, clauses, and appositives.

The men ⊙ putting up the fence ⊙ are with the local building supply company.

People ⊙ that drink too much ⊙ often have serious family problems.

John Gardner's book ⊙ *Grendel* ⊙ received many favorable reviews.

6.   Do not use a comma before the first item in a series or after the last item.

Barbara reads such books as ⊙ *Evelina, Emma,* and *Middlemarch.*

Not surprisingly, Barbara is an intelligent, sophisticated, and poised ⊙ woman.

12

Semicolons

The semicolon is used between equal grammatical constructions.

1. Use the semicolon between main clauses not connected by *and, or, nor, but, yet,* or *so.*

> *The Music Man* is a fine musical; its best-known song is "Seventy-Six Trombones."

> Most employees are covered by medical insurance; however, relatively few are covered by dental insurance.

2. Use semicolons to separate main clauses that themselves contain commas.

> Betty Collins, a most unlikely candidate, was nominated on the first ballot; but, she told reporters, the party would be pleased with her nomination when she won the election in November.
>
> > The coordinate conjunction *but* indicates the break between the main clauses. Since the break between main clauses is more important than the breaks indicated by the four commas, the conjunction needs a semicolon before it to stress this importance.

Though there is no absolute rule for when the coordinate conjunction needs a semicolon before it at the break between main clauses, an acceptable practice would be to use the semicolon before a coordinate conjunction connecting main clauses when there is a total of two commas in the main clauses. This could mean two commas in the first main clause, two commas in the second main clause, or one comma in the first main clause and one comma in the second.

Two commas in first main clause: Andrew Carnegie, as well as John Rockefeller, made a fortune from the American capitalistic system; and Carnegie became one of America's most famous philanthropists.

Two commas in second main clause: Quite a few writers rebel against establishment values; but many of these authors, surprisingly enough, are shocked when the establishment rejects their revolutionary ideas.

One comma in both the first and second main clauses: Evaluating the track conditions closely, the trainer decided the horse should run; but the valuable animal received a debilitating injury, unfortunately.

3.   Use semicolons to separate items in a series that itself contains commas.

Mr. William Engel was accompanied by his son John Engel, a buyer for Nichol's Mills; his daughter Joan Shaw, an executive with Person's Bank; and his wife, a board member of the Utah Power and Light Company.

A reminder: Do *not* use the semicolon to connect unequal grammatical constructions.

Having judged all the evidence available to him at the courthouse; James decided that the real estate cooperative was a rip-off.
    The semicolon is used *incorrectly* to connect a participial phrase to a main clause.

Although the governor said he feared the decision would contribute to inflation; he kept salaries at the same level as the previous year.
    The semicolon is used *incorrectly* to connect a subordinate clause to a main clause.

The incumbent tried hard to get the votes of all state employees; a task that he could never accomplish.
    The semicolon is used *incorrectly* to connect a main clause to a noun modified by an adjective clause.

13

Apostrophes

The apostrophe helps to steamline expressions that otherwise would be clumsy and wordy:

> the hat of the girl
> the bats of the boys
> the plays of Seneca
>> *Girl's hat, boys' bats,* and *Seneca's plays* would be much better.

English expressions containing apostrophes to indicate possession can be rewritten in phrases consisting of nouns followed by prepositional phrases. Restructuring the expressions in such phrases often helps clarify meaning. For example, if you were asked to put the apostrophe where it was needed in the expression *the guests attire,* you would need to know whether the expression meant "the attire of the guest" or "the attire of the guests." *The guest's attire* means the attire of one guest, and *the guests' attire* means the attire of more than one guest. Once you have mentally restructured the expression in its correct form (noun plus prepositional phrase), you simply put the apostrophe where it belongs.

Also, many expressions containing apostrophes can be rewritten as nouns followed by prepositional phrases, but these expressions are not necessarily possessive. For instance, the expression *tomorrow's assignment* does not mean tomorrow possesses the assignment. Similarly, the expression *a good day's work* does not mean the day owns the work. Nevertheless, such an expression as *tomorrow's assignment* can still be rewritten as a noun plus a prepositional phrase: *the assignment for tomorrow.* Remembering that such nonpossessive uses of the apostrophe can be written out in the same manner as possessive constructions should help you better understand the use of the apostrophe.

Sometimes apostrophes are used to indicate omissions, and sometimes they are used to form plurals. To simplify the uses of the apostrophe, we have divided this chapter into three sections: possession, omission, and plurals.

Possession

1. To form the possessive of most singular nouns not ending in -*s*, add an apostrophe and -*s*.

the mayor's son
the team's coach
the student's test

2. To form the possessive of singular nouns of one syllable ending in -*s*, add an apostrophe and -*s*.

the boss's secretary
Keats's poem
James's car

3. To form the possessive of singular nouns of more than one syllable ending in -*s*, add just an apostrophe.

the mattress' label
Socrates' philosophy
Aeschylus' trilogy

4. To form the possessive of plural nouns ending in -*s*, add only an apostrophe.

the players' contracts
the Smiths' house
the Joneses' vacation

5. To form the possessive of plural nouns not ending in -*s*, add an apostrophe and -*s*.

the men's organization
the children's magazine
the women's project

6.   Use an apostrophe and -*s* to form the possessive of indefinite pronouns.

> anybody's
> everybody's
> someone's

But notice that no apostrophe is needed with personal pronouns, relative pronouns, or possessive pronouns.

> ours
> > **not** our's
>
> yours
> > **not** your's
>
> hers
> > **not** her's
>
> whose
> > **not** who's
>
> its
> > **not** it's

7.   Add an apostrophe and -*s* to the last word to indicate the possessive of compounds and word groups.

> my mother-in-law's bookstore
> anyone else's rights

8.   Use an apostrophe to indicate authorship.

> Herman Melville's *Moby Dick*
> Ernest Hemingway's "The Killers"
> Euripides' *Iphigenia in Tauris*

9.   Use an apostrophe and -*s* with a noun or with an indefinite pronoun preceding a gerund.

> Diana Nyad's swimming from the Bahamas to Florida required unbelievable endurance.

> Someone's stealing the Christmas bell upset the townspeople.

10.   Add an apostrophe and -*s* to the last name in a series to denote possession by two or more jointly.

> Betty and Sue's piano
> Lewis and Clark's expedition

11.   Add an apostrophe and -*s* to each name to denote individual ownership.

> John's and Robert's cars
> Pam Smith's and Elizabeth Hardy's pianos

12.   Use the form accepted by tradition and law in indicating geographical terms, as well as names of firms, organizations, institutions, clubs, and titles.

> Harpers Ferry
> Rutgers University
> Lions Club
> King's College
> Gilbert's Fine Furniture, Inc.

Omission

1.   Use an apostrophe to mark the omission of a letter or letters in a contraction.

> don't   (do not)
> can't   (cannot)
> I'm   (I am)
> o'clock   (of the clock)
> it's   (it is)
> who's   (who is)

Be sure to put the apostrophe in the proper place.

> they're, **not** theyr'e
> didn't, **not** did'nt

Do not confuse the contractions *it's* and *who's* with the possessive pronouns *its* and *whose*.

> It's a beautiful day.
>> *It's* means "it is."

> The old car needs its engine overhauled.

> Who's at the front door?
>> *Who's* means "who is."

> Whose books did you buy?

2. Use apostrophes to indicate the pronunciation of dialectical speech.

> Watch you w'en your gittin' all you want. Fattenin' hogs ain't in luck.
>> *Joel Chandler Harris*

3. Add an apostrophe where a figure or figures have been omitted.

> class of '41 (1941)
> spirit of '76 (1776)

Plurals

1. Use the apostrophe and -*s* to indicate the plurals of letters used as letters.

> His *l*'s look like *i*'s.
> There are four *i*'s and four *s*'s in *Mississippi*.

2. Use the apostrophe and -*s* to indicate the plurals of words used as words.

> Mary often confuses her *and*'s and her *an*'s.
> It is hard to tell the difference between his *ploy*'s and his *play*'s.

3.   Use an apostrophe and *-s* to indicate the plurals of figures used as figures.

> The printer in the school shop has no more *3*'s.
> The teacher writes *9*'s that look like *7*'s.

4.   Use the apostrophe and *-s* to indicate the plurals of symbols and of some abbreviations.

> That model typewriter's *#*'s and *$*'s are very close to each other.

> One English professor at Harvard has four *M.A.*'s and two *Ph.D.*'s.

Be careful not to use apostrophes carelessly when the noun is plural and not possessive.

> The Joneses are good neighbors.

14

Quotation Marks

Unlike the rules concerning some marks of punctuation, the rules concerning quotation marks are fairly well standardized. The main rule is always, "Quotation marks come in pairs." Whenever you use an opening set of quotation marks, you must remember that a closing set will be required.

Since quotation marks serve more than one purpose, this chapter is divided into four parts: direct quotations, titles, special sense, and with other marks of punctuation.

Direct Quotations

1. Use double quotation marks to enclose direct quotations. Capitalize the first letter of the first word of a quoted sentence.

> Plutarch said, "It is indeed a desirable thing to be well descended, but the glory belongs to our ancestors."

Do not capitalize the first letter of the first word of a quotation if what is quoted is not a complete sentence and the letter would not ordinarily be capitalized.

> Plutarch said that it is fine for us to be descended from famous people but added that the fame "belongs to our ancestors."

Do not use quotation marks to set off an indirect quotation. An indirect quotation reflects the original thought but is not in the exact words of the original. Indirect quotations are often introduced by the word *that*.

> Plutarch said that it was fine for us to be descended from

famous people but added that the fame belonged to those who earned it.

2.   Use single quotation marks to enclose a quotation within a quotation.

> John said, "Many American soldiers in Vietnam did not agree with Nathan Hale's words, 'I only regret that I have but one life to lose for my country.'"

3.   With a quotation within a quotation within a quotation, double quotation marks are used first, then single quotation marks, and then double quotation marks again.

> "It is a brave man indeed," Jonathan said, "who believes Lieutenant Edward's sentiment: 'Every good soldier agrees with Nathan Hale's words, "I only regret that I have but one life to lose for my country."'"

Quotation marks should not get any more involved than quotations within quotations. When the sentence would be more complicated than that, it should be rewritten.

Note: If you read books or magazines printed in the British Isles or in British territories, you will find that the use of double quotation marks and single quotation marks is exactly the reverse of what has been explained in this chapter. American usage, however, does not permit the use of single quotation marks by themselves except in headlines.

4.   The preferred way of reproducing long quotations is to omit the enclosing quotation marks and indent the entire passage of the quotation about a half-inch. In a typed paper, you should double-space the indented quotation.

> It is interesting that—like Allen Tate, T. S. Eliot, and Ezra Pound—Randall Jarrell never wrote a defense of poetry for the people who felt it needed one. He felt strongly that
>
> > poetry does not need to be defended, any more than air or food needs to be defended; poetry—using the word in its widest sense, the only sense in which it is important—has been an indispensable part of any culture we know anything

about. Human life without some form of poetry is not
human life but animal existence.[1]

Because he believed poetry was necessary for human existence, he refused to jump on the bandwagon and condemn
modern poetry because of its complexity.

5.   A two-line quotation from a poem can be handled in either of
two ways.

The quotation may be incorporated into the text by enclosing
it in quotation marks and using a slash to indicate the end of the
first line.

Alexander Pope said in his *Essay in Criticism*, "A little
learning is a dangerous thing;/ Drink deep, or taste not the
Pierian spring." There are many such memorable statements in the poetic essay.

The quotation may be set off from the text and reproduced exactly as it appears in the original (with no quotation marks employed that are not in the original).

Alexander Pope said in his *Essay in Criticism*,

A little learning is a dangerous thing;
Drink deep, or taste not the Pierian spring.

There are many such memorable statements in the poetic
essay.

6.   Longer passages from poems must be set off from the text and
reproduced exactly as they are found in the original.

The well-known Scottish poet Robert Burns once wrote:

My love is like a red red rose
That's newly sprung in June:
My love is like the melodie
That's sweetly play'd in tune.

Many English teachers quote the stanza when they are ex-
plaining similes to their students.

---

1. Randall Jarrell, "The Obscurity of the Poet," *Partisan Review* 18 (Jan.–Feb.
1951): 67.

7.   In dialogue the standard practice is to begin a new paragraph with each change in speaker.

> "I just don't see how Barbara can sit in front of the TV set all afternoon and watch soap operas."
> "I know what you mean. But Jane does the same thing. Sometimes she gets so caught up in the stories that she forgets to pick the kids up at school."

Remember to set off such expressions as *he said, she replied,* and *he asked* with commas.

> Ellen asked, "Will Paul come to the meeting?"
> "Paul cannot attend the meeting today," Jane replied.
> "If Paul would come," Ellen said, "we could finish this project today."

Titles

Books and newspapers do not handle titles the same way. Newspapers use practically no italics at all, whereas books generally use italics for separate publications. The rule presented in this section reflects the usage of reputable book publishers. The general rule is to italicize (underline) the title of a long work and to enclose the title of a short work in quotation marks. Use quotation marks to enclose the titles of newspaper and magazine articles, essays, short stories, short poems, short musical works, and subdivisions of books.

> "Dover Beach" is Matthew Arnold's best-known poem.

> "The Unparalleled Adventure of One Hans Pfaall" is an interesting short story by Edgar Allan Poe.

> One of T. S. Eliot's most famous essays is "Tradition and the Individual Talent."

> A series entitled "The Community College: A Better Way" appeared in the *Montgomery Herald.*

> The first big hit in America by the Beatles was "I Want to Hold Your Hand."

Part 2 of Herman Wouk's *War and Remembrance* is entitled "Midway."

To Indicate Special Sense

1. Use quotation marks to call attention to an unusual word or
phrase, a technical term, or a slang or dialectical expression that
differs in style from the context.

> The minister knew he was "right on" with his advice to the
> young.

> An "erg" is a unit of energy.

2. Use quotation marks to suggest that a word or phrase is being
used ironically.

> Jim's "valuable" prize turned out to be a cheap watch.

> The "easy" economics exam caused Jerry to graduate a se-
> mester behind his classmates.

Because enclosing an expression in quotation marks really makes
it stand out, be sure not to overuse quotation marks to indicate
that a word or phrase is used in a special sense. To overuse the de-
vice merely weakens its effectiveness.

With Other Marks of Punctuation

1. Place the period and the comma inside the quotation marks.

> "You know," the Senator said, "I think I'll run for president."
> "Please get off my foot," Kathy asked nicely.

2. Place the colon and the semicolon outside the quotation
marks.

> One of Poe's best stories is "The Gold-Bug"; the story takes
> place in South Carolina.

> There are four important characters in "The Open Boat":
> the cook, the captain, the oiler, and the correspondent.

3. Place the question mark and the exclamation point inside the quotation marks when they apply to the quoted matter.

Barbara asked, "Are you ready?"

Did he ask, "What is reality?"

"Tackle him! Tackle him!" the coach shouted from the sidelines.

"Can we stay here?" she asked.
>   Notice in the last two sentences that no comma follows a question mark or an exclamation point.

4. Place the question mark and the exclamation point outside the quotation marks when they apply to the whole sentence.

Stop singing "Dixie"!
Do you like "Yankee Doodle"?

Sometimes the proper use of quotation marks can be complicated. For instance, the following sentence contains a quotation within a quotation; the overall sentence is a question but the quotation within a quotation is a statement.

Bob asked his neighbor, "Did my wife say, 'I'm leaving'?"

15

Capitalization and Italics

Capitalization

Capitalization usage changes with time, meaning, and purpose. At best, capitalization rules serve only as guides. Since it is important, however, to be as consistent as possible, use capital letters only for a specific purpose and with a particular rule in mind.

In this section the rules of capitalization are divided into three units to make them easier to remember: (1) mechanics; (2) places, times, and kinds; and (3) government and social, publishing and personification.

Mechanics

1.   Capitalize the first word of every sentence.

The amateur defeated the professional in the pro-am tournament.

2.   Capitalize a word or the first word of a phrase that stands alone like a sentence.

Thanks.
Objection overruled.

3.   Capitalize the first word of a direct quotation within a sentence (but not if the quotation is a fragment).

Kahlil Gibran said, "Let there be spaces in your togetherness."

Kahlil Gibran says you must have "spaces in your togetherness."

4.   Capitalize the first word of each line of poetry (unless it isn't capitalized in the original).

> The woods are lovely, dark and deep
> But I have promises to keep,
> And miles to go before I sleep.
> > *Robert Frost*

But some poets prefer not to capitalize:

> it's just like a coffin's
> inside when you die,
> pretentious and
> shiny and
> not too wide
> > *e. e. cummings*

5.   Capitalize a common noun when it is used alone as a well-known short form of a specific proper name.

> the Gulf (Gulf of Mexico)
> the Capitol (in Washington, D.C.)

6.   Capitalize the interjection *O* and the pronoun *I*.

Come forward, O dear friends; I need your help.

7.   Capitalize all proper nouns and adjectives.

> Faculty Senate
> Surry Community College
> Louisville Country Club
> Lookout Dam

But notice:

> a college
> an avenue
> a dam
> a democracy

8.   Capitalize the first word and any nouns in the salutation of a letter.

Gentlemen
Dear Mr. Smith
My dear Gloria

But only the first word of the complimentary close is capitalized:

Very truly yours
Sincerely yours

9.   Capitalize calendar designations.

Monday
August
Thanksgiving Day

But notice:

twentieth century
winter

10.   Capitalize the abbreviations of many titles and degrees and some common one- or two-letter abbreviations.

James Alfred Draughn, Ph.D.
Theodore N. Swaim, Jr.
TV, CB, F (Fahrenheit)

11.   Capitalize the numerals used to refer to organizations or to periods of time. Spell out numerals preceding a name. Often, numerals following a name are put in Roman numerals.

First World War
Second Army
World War II
Edward VII
Fifty-first Congress

12.   Capitalize expressions of time such as *A.M.*, *P.M.*, *A.D.*, and *B.C.* (Some writers prefer not to use capital letters for *a.m.* and *p.m.*)

55 B.C.
6:20 A.M.

Places, Times, and Kinds

13.   Capitalize geographical terms.

> Hudson River
> Irish Sea
> Pike's Peak
> Rocky Mountains
> Lake Erie

But notice:

> the Erie and Huron lakes

14.   Capitalize descriptive terms used to designate a definite region or locality.

> the North Atlantic States
> the South
> Eastern Hemisphere
> the Promised Land

Directional parts of states are not capitalized, however.

> eastern Kentucky
> southern Idaho

Also, compass points are not capitalized when indicating direction.

> The Smiths drove west for ten miles and then headed northwest for the next twenty-five miles.

15.   Capitalize the names of specific streets, roads, highways, toll roads, etc.

> Highway 66
> Road 2249
> West Virginia Turnpike

16.   Capitalize proper names.

> John Conklin
> Spain
> Paris

17. Capitalize the derivatives of proper names used with a proper meaning.

> Miltonic style
> Jeffersonian democracy
> Spanish
> Parisian
> American

Words derived from proper names but that now have independent meanings are not capitalized.

> china (meaning *porcelain*)
> pasteurize
> bohemian
> volt

18. Capitalize nouns of kinship when used as substitutes for proper names.

> I would like to introduce you to Dad.

But do not capitalize nouns of kinship that are preceded by an article or a possessive.

> She is my mother.

19. Capitalize a course of study only if the name of the subject is derived from a proper noun or if you are referring to a specific course title.

> French
> German
> Piaget's Theory of Cognition
> History 101
> Shorthand II

But:

> history
> shorthand

20.   Capitalize the word *the* only when it is part of an official name or title.

> The Hague
> *The Tempest*

But the word *the* is not generally capitalized in references to newspapers, magazines, vessels, and company names:

> the *Atlantic Monthly*
> the *U.S.S. America*
> the *Winston-Salem Journal*
> the Fuji Film Co.

21.   Capitalize the scientific name of a genus but not the name of a species.

> *Acer saccharinum* (genus and species)

22.   Capitalize religious feast, festival, and fast days as well as historic events and eras.

> Feast of the Passover
> the Renaissance
> Yom Kippur
> Christmas Day
> Battle of Salamis
> Korean War
> the Middle Ages
> the Treaty of Versailles

23.   Capitalize names for God or the Trinity, both nouns and adjectives, and pronouns referring to the Deity.

> the Messiah
> Our Father
> His mercy

24. Capitalize words that refer to the Bible or other sacred writings.

> Holy Bible
> Genesis
> Koran

Government and Social, Publishing and Personifying

25. Capitalize the names of administrative, legislative, and judicial bodies and departments.

> House of Representatives
> Supreme Court
> Department of Commerce
> General Assembly of North Carolina

26. Capitalize the names of organizations, political parties, alliances, institutions, religious groups, races, movements, classes, nationalities, athletic teams, civic groups, etc.

> Lions Club
> Young Men's Christian Association
> Republican party
> Princeton University
> Catholics
> Jews
> Women's Liberation Movement
> Dallas Cowboys

But:

> democracy
> club

27. Capitalize any titles preceding a person's name.

> President Kennedy
> King Charles
> Ambassador Smith
> Professor Wiles

28.   Capitalize a common-noun title immediately following a name or used alone as a substitute for it to indicate preeminence or distinction.

> Jim Rawlings, Governor
> the President (of the United States)
> the King (referring to a specific one)
> the Pope

29.   Capitalize the first and last words of the titles of books, articles, student compositions, etc., and capitalize all other important words (nouns, verbs, adjectives, and adverbs). Do not capitalize articles (*a, an, the*) or short (four letters or less) prepositions or conjunctions.

> *Gone with the Wind*
> *A Raisin in the Sun*
> "An Analysis of Roderick Usher"

But notice:

> "The Man Against the Sky"
> *Desire Under the Elms*
>> The prepositions *against* and *under* contain five letters or more.

30.   Capitalize trade names, variety names, and names of market grades.

> Corning Ware (trade name)
> Golden Delicious apple (variety)
> USDA Choice (market grade)

31.   Capitalize all personifications. (Personification is the granting of human attributes to abstract ideas and inanimate objects.)

> Suddenly and unexpectedly, Death crept into the room during the night.
> The Chair recognizes the representative from Guilford County.

Italics (Underlining)

There is no definitive set of rules for the use of italic type. Different publishers follow different rules. Nevertheless, the rules presented in this chapter generally reflect the usage recommended by the *U.S. Government Printing Office Style Manual* and most authorities. In typewritten and handwritten papers you should underline in all cases where printers use italics.

1.   Italicize all titles of separate publications (books, magazines, newspapers, plays, long musical compositions, long poems, etc.).

> *U.S. Government Printing Office Style Manual* (book)
> *Rosencrantz and Guildenstern Are Dead* (play)
> *Paradise Lost* (epic poem)
> *La Bohème* (opera, long musical work)
> *Moby Dick* (novel)
> *U.S. News & World Report* (magazine)
> the *Chicago Tribune* (newspaper)

2.   Italicize the names of ships, trains, aircraft, and spacecraft.

> The *Queen Elizabeth II* is a beautiful ship.
> Lindbergh's *Spirit of St. Louis* was small and fragile.
> The moon-mission of *Apollo II* will never be forgotten.

3.   Italicize the titles of motion pictures and works of art.

> *Star Wars* was a movie with magnificent special effects.
>
> Michelangelo's *David* is one of the most famous sculptures in the world.
>
> Leonardo da Vinci's *Mona Lisa* is perhaps the most famous painting in the world.

4.   Italicize the Latin names of genus and species.

> *Osmunda cinnamomea* (cinnamon fern)
> *Canis familiaris* (dog)

5.   Italicize foreign words and expressions.

raison d'être (French for "reason for being")
e pluribus unum (Latin for "from many, one")

Note: Many foreign words and expressions are so commonly used they are said to be Anglicized; such words and expressions are not italicized:

patio (Spanish)
hors d'oeuvre (French)
bona fide (Latin)

6.   Italicize a letter, word, number, or expression when it is spoken of as such or used as an illustration.

The *i*'s on that make of typewriter look like *l*'s.
The words *adapt* and *adopt* confuse many readers.
Please form your *Z*'s and *3*'s distinctly.

7.   Italicize sparingly to emphasize a word or expression.

Write all essays in *ink*!
Do not overuse italicizing in this manner.

16

Abbreviations and Numbers

Abbreviations

Standard English usage permits few abbreviations. As might be expected, there is little consistency in the abbreviations it does accept. Also, the acceptability of abbreviations varies according to the purpose of the writing. For instance, a chart in a technical report and the bibliography of a scholarly article will use far more abbreviations than the standard prose of most popular magazines and books written for a general audience. Naturally, the audience aimed at will largely determine the acceptability of abbreviations. Technical matter aimed at specialists who share a similar background and who are expected to know the jargon of the field contains numerous abbreviations. In fact, the abbreviations, symbols, and equations of some technical writing are practically a form of shorthand. On the other hand, abbreviations are kept to a minimum in popular magazines such as *Time, Newsweek*, and *Reader's Digest*. In these magazines the purpose is clarity. You too should have clarity as a goal. You do not want to use any abbreviations that might confuse your reader.

Though lists of acceptable abbreviations might differ greatly from one magazine to another, some conventions in abbreviating have developed over the years. This chapter presents the conventions most often accepted in standard English writing for non-technical audiences.

1. Use the abbreviations *Mr., Mrs., Miss, Ms., St.,* and *Dr.* whenever these titles precede a proper name.

Dr. Alice Smith
Mr. Jones

Mrs. Alistair
Ms. Frances Ingram
St. Christopher

2.   Use the abbreviations *Gen., Sgt., Prof., Gov., Rev., Hon., Sen., Rep.,* and *Capt.* if the title is followed by a first name or an initial as well as a surname.

Gen. George Patton
Rev. J. Hutton
Prof. H. Kissinger

But:

Captain Adams
Sergeant Brown

3.   Use the abbreviations *Jr.* and *Sr.* when preceded by a proper name.

William E. Edmonds, Jr.
Edward J. Pendleton, Sr.

4.   Use the abbreviations *D.D., Ph.D., M.A., B.A., M.D.,* and *C.P.A.* when preceded by a proper name or alone if the context is clear.

June R. Mandell, Ph.D.
William C. Ludwig, C.P.A.
He earned an M.A. degree before he sat for the C.P.A. exam.

5.   Use the abbreviations *Co., Corp., Inc., Bros., Ltd.* and symbols such as the ampersand (&) in describing business firms only when the abbreviations are part of the legally authorized name.

Grosset & Dunlap, Inc.
Jones Bros. & Co.
Radio Corp. of America
A & P Company

6.   The abbreviations *i.e., e.g., cf., et al., etc.,* and *vs.* or *v.* may be used in any type of writing.

i.e.   (that is)   et al.   (and others)

e.g.   (for example)   etc.   (and so forth)
cf.   (compare)   vs. or v.   (versus)

The artist brought several examples of his craft, e.g., silver
pitchers and pewter sconces.

7. Use the following abbreviations for states when they immediately follow any capitalized geographic term. Alaska, Hawaii,
Idaho, Iowa, Maine, Ohio, and Utah are spelled out in full. Do not
abbreviate the name of the state when it stands alone.

Ala.	Kans.	N. Dak.	S.C.
Ariz.	Ky.	Nebr.	S. Dak.
Ark.	La.	Nev.	Tenn.
Calif.	Mass.	N.H.	Tex.
Colo.	Md.	N.J.	Va.
Conn.	Mich.	N. Mex.	Vt.
Del.	Minn.	N.Y.	Wash.
Fla.	Miss.	Okla.	Wis.
Ga.	Mo.	Oreg.	W. Va.
Ill.	Mont.	Pa.	Wyo.
Ind.	N.C.	R.I.	

Albany, N.Y.
Nashville, Tenn.
Portland, Maine
Provo, Utah
Little Rock, Ark.

But:

She was born in South Carolina.

8. Use the abbreviation *U.S.S.R.* (Union of Soviet Socialist Re-
publics), but spell out the names of all other countries.

in Brazil
in London, England
in the U.S.S.R.

9.   Use the abbreviation *U.S.* as an adjective but not as a noun.

U.S. Navy
U.S. Government Printing Office
in the United States

10.   Use the abbreviations *A.D., B.C., A.M., P.M., no.* or *No.*, and the symbol *$* only with dates or figures.

A.D. 1066
350 B.C.
4:50 P.M.
$100
No. 3

11.   Use the abbreviation *D.C.* for District of Columbia.

Washington, D.C.

12.   Use abbreviations for things normally referred to by their capitalized initials.

CB
TV

13.   Use commonly accepted acronyms (words derived from the initial letters or syllables of successive parts of a term).

Amoco (American Oil Company)
UNESCO (United Nations Educational, Scientific, and Cultural Organization)

14.   Spell out months, days of the week, and units of measurement.

Monday
September
Mary is nearly six feet tall.
163 pounds

15. Spell out the words *street, avenue, boulevard, road, square, court, park, mount,* and *river* used as an essential part of proper names.

> Fifth Avenue
> Hampton Court
> Washington Square
> East Boulevard

16. Spell out the names of courses of study and the words for *page, chapter, volume, part, book,* and *canto.*

> I studied physical education and chemistry.
> page 15
> Chapter 3
> canto XXXI

17. Spell out first names.

> George Washington
>   not Geo. Washington
> William Penn
>   not Wm. Penn
> Thomas Jefferson
>   not Thos. Jefferson

18. For an abbreviation that is not generally known, write out the full form in parentheses immediately following its first use.

> b.h.p. (brake horsepower)
> F.S.L.N. (Sandinista National Liberation Front)

19. Do not use a period after chemical symbols.

> $C_8H_{15}N$
> H_2O

20. Do not use a period after initials of military services and specific military terms.

USN	United States Navy
MP	Military Police
MIA	Missing in Action

AWOL   Absent Without Leave
PX   Post Exchange

21. Do not use a period after the acronyms of certain governmental agencies or call letters of television and radio stations.

DOE   Department of Energy
FBI   Federal Bureau of Investigation
CIA   Central Intelligence Agency
WXII   television station call letters
WB4EIV   amateur radio operator's call letters

Numbers

There seems to be a growing trend these days toward the use of more figures in writing. It is a known fact that readers can comprehend figures more quickly than they can comprehend the written-out forms of numbers. And, of course, figures are vastly preferable in much technical and scientific material. Nevertheless, some rules governing the use of figures are applicable in most standard English prose written for the general reader; those rules are presented in this chapter.

1. Use figures for numbers that require more than two words to spell out.

153
4,289

But notice:

twenty-four
ninety-six
ten

2. Use figures for time designations used with A.M., P.M., B.C., and A.D.

8:01 A.M.
55 B.C.
11:53 P.M.
A.D. 1066

But **not:**

> ten A.M.
> thirty-three B.C.

3.   Use figures in addresses.

> Route 2
> 1128 Belgrade Drive
> P. O. Box 531
> Room 374

4.   Use figures for most dates but not all.

> May 1849
> January 5, 1946 or 5 January 1946
> August ninth or the ninth of August or August 9 or August 9th
> the sixties or the 1960s or the 1960's
> the twentieth century
> 1600 or 1632–1638 or 1632–38
> from 1941 to 1945

But **not:**

> May, 1849
> > The comma is not needed.

> January 5th, 1946
> > Do not use *th* when the year follows.

> from 1941–1945
> > *From* must be accompanied by the complementary word *to*.

5.   Use figures for serial numbers.

> Newsletter 63
> page 154
> Chapter 4
> paragraph 2
> Document 12

6. Use figures (normally Roman numerals) to differentiate kings, emperors, and popes with the same names.

> Edward VIII
> Charles V
> Elizabeth II
> Boniface VI

7. Use figures (generally Roman numerals) in denoting vehicles.

> *Courageous II*
> *Pioneer I*
> *Apollo IX*

8. Use figures (Roman numerals) to designate family members of the same name.

> Ralston M. Ounce, III
> John R. Dobbins, IV

9. Use figures to designate local branches of labor unions and fraternal lodges.

> Teamsters Local 391
> American Legion Post 266

10. Use figures to designate state and interstate highways.

> North Carolina 52
> Interstate 77

11. Use figures with decimals, degrees, percentages, money, and proportion.

> 35.6 inches
> longitude 51°05′01″ W
> 33 percent
> $912.69
> odds of 4 to 1

12.   Use figures with game scores, election results, statistics, and items in a series.

> a score of 50 to 6
> a vote of 321 to 9 against
> 4 hammers, 7 screwdrivers, and 1,268 nails

13.   Use figures in parentheses to repeat numbers in legal or commercial writing.

> The cashier keeps two hundred (200) dollars of ready cash on hand.

> or

> The cashier keeps two hundred dollars ($200) of ready cash on hand.

14.   Large round numbers may be either spelled out or put in figures.

> thirty million dollars
> $30,000,000
> $30 million

15.   Spell out numbers beginning sentences.

> Ninety men volunteered for the assignment.
> Five percent of the Conservative Party are actually Marxists.

When possible, rewrite sentences so that numbers do not come at the beginning.

16.   Spell out ordinal numbers preceding the noun of successive dynasties, governments, and governing bodies.

> Third Reich
> Eighty-second Congress
> Twelfth Dynasty

17.   Spell out ordinal numbers less than one hundred that designate political divisions and military units.

> Fifth Congressional District
> Third Ward
> Ninety-fourth Precinct
> Second Army
> Forty-fifth Regiment
> Seventeenth Battalion

18.   Spell out numbered streets under one hundred.

> Fifth Avenue
> Thirty-second Street

19.   Spell out numbers designating churches or religious organizations.

> First Presbyterian Church
> Seventh-day Adventists

20.   Spell out numbers preceding the expression *o'clock*.

> eight o'clock

17

Other Marks of Punctuation

In this chapter we present the punctuation marks that have not previously been discussed. The punctuation marks in this chapter are no less important than other punctuation marks that may have more rules governing their usage. In fact, some of the marks discussed here are so specialized that any incorrect use of them could confuse your readers.

Periods

1. Use a period to mark the end of a declarative sentence (one that makes a statement) or a mildly imperative sentence (one that expresses a command or makes a request).

> Matt Davis is the best blocker on the team.
> > The sentence makes a statement.

> Please close the door.
> > The sentence makes a request.

> Open the glove compartment and get my gloves.
> > The sentence expresses commands.

But a strongly imperative sentence needs an exclamation point.

> Put your hands over your head and lean against the wall!

2. Use a period to mark the end of an indirect question. Words such as *when* and *what* often introduce questions that are asked so indirectly that no question mark is necessary.

155

> The Dean asked me when I could come by and speak with him.
>
> Martha asked what Bob had said about her.

3. Use a period to mark the end of a polite request, even if it is worded as a question. Business letters often reflect this use of the period. When a businessperson asks a question in a letter, the intent is often more a mild imperative than a question. Also, in such cases the answer is generally assumed to be *yes*.

> Will you reply by return mail.
>
> Will you see that the shipment is adequately insured.

4. Use a period for most abbreviations.

> Mrs.
>
> Dr.
>
> P.M.
>
> A.M.
>
> etc.
>
> e.g.

Use only one period if a declarative sentence ends with an abbreviation.

> The new economics professor is from Washington, D.C.

Use a question mark or an exclamation point after the abbreviation period if an interrogative sentence (one that asks a direct question) or an exclamatory sentence (one that expresses strong feeling or surprise) ends with an abbreviation.

> Is the pitcher from Charlotte, N.C.?

> Don't hop a train to Chicago, Ill.!

Use whatever punctuation mark would normally be used to follow an abbreviation period inside the sentence.

> Some writers use many abbreviations such as *i.e., e.g.,* and *etc.*; other writers, however, do not favor such Latin abbreviations.

5. Use a period to separate dollars from cents in writing figures.

> $1.29
>
> $36.94

6.   Use the period as a decimal point in writing figures.

98.6°
16.8 percent
$15.6 million

Leaders and Ellipses

There are several instances where "multiple periods" are employed in writing.

Some printers use leaders (a line of periods) in the table of contents of a book to guide the reader's eye from a chapter title to the page on which the chapter begins.

Some printers use three centered periods (or asterisks) to indicate the omission of long passages (a paragraph, a page, or even several chapters). In the following passage, the second paragraph of a three-paragraph letter from Samuel Johnson to James Macpherson has been left out.

> Mr. James Macpherson—I received your foolish and impudent note. Whatever insult is offered me I will do my best to repel, and what I cannot do for myself the law will do for me. I will not desist from detecting what I think a cheat, from any fear of the menaces of a Ruffian.
>
> . . .
>
> But however I may despise you, I reverence truth and if you can prove the genuineness of the work I will confess it. Your rage I defy, your abilities since your Homer are not so formidable, and what I have heard of your morals disposes me to pay regard not to what you shall say, but to what you can prove.
>
> You may print this if you will,
> *Samuel Johnson*

The most common use of multiple periods is the ellipsis. The ellipsis mark is three spaced periods in a row. It is sometimes, as in mathematics, used to indicate that a series, pattern, or listing continues on beyond the last item cited.

The boy counted to one hundred: 1, 2, 3, 4 . . .

Sometimes an ellipsis is used to indicate the passage of time.

It was a beautiful morning . . . a cloudy afternoon . . . a stormy evening.

By far the most important use of the ellipsis mark, however, is to indicate that part of a quotation has been left out. Since quotations are normally supposed to be reproduced exactly as they appeared in the original, the ellipsis mark is important in that it lets you alter the quotation by omitting part of it. You should familiarize yourself with the following two rules:

1. If the omission occurs at the beginning or in the middle of a sentence, use three periods.

". . . Wanting both government and liberty the writer . . . pointed out the relationship between the two."

Sometimes the ellipses at the beginning of a quotation are omitted.

2. If the last part of a quoted sentence is omitted or if entire sentences of a quoted passage are omitted, add a fourth period.

Original quotation: Literature is my Utopia. Here I am not disfranchised. No barrier of the senses shuts me out from the sweet, gracious discourse of my book-friends. They talk to me without embarrassment or awkwardness.
—*Helen Keller*

Quotation with ellipses: Literature is my Utopia. . . . No barrier of the senses shuts me out from the . . . discourse of my book-friends. They talk to me without embarrassment or awkwardness.

Ellipses should not be used to alter the meaning of the original source. If a reviewer says, "I do not think the book is very good," it would be misleading of you to reproduce the quotation leaving out the word *not*, "I do . . . think the book is very good."

Brackets

Like ellipses, brackets can be useful in reproducing quotations. Ellipses permit us to omit words from quotations; brackets permit us to add words. Do not confuse brackets [ ] with parentheses ( ). Parentheses are used to enclose parenthetical material in your own work, whereas brackets are used to add your own parenthetical comments, corrections, and additions to the passage you are quoting.

1.   Use brackets to enclose an explanation that is inserted in quoted material and that is not part of the original text.

> James Macke wrote, "She [Emily Dickinson] is the best female poet America has produced."

> The newspaper reported, "Sebastian Coe now holds the world's record for each leg in the Triple Crown [800 meters, 1,500 meters, and the mile]."

2.   Use brackets enclosing the Latin word *sic* (meaning "thus") following errors in fact, spelling, punctuation, or grammar to indicate that you know the errors are present.

> The book stated, "Abraham Lincoln was assassinated on April 14, 1965 [*sic*]."

> The student wrote "The English coarse [*sic*] was very difficult."

3.   You can correct some errors in the original text by enclosing the correction in brackets.

> The division manager wrote the owner, "You should get Roger Boyd inste[a]d of Bill Tompkins."

> The newspaper summarized the election results with the headline, "McDonald To Be New Pres[id]ent."

Colons

The colon is a rather formal mark of punctuation. Some writers prefer not to use it. Nevertheless, there are some situations where the colon is the most appropriate mark of punctuation to use.

1. Use the colon to introduce a series of examples or a list of items.

> There are three kinds of extrasensory perception: telepathy, clairvoyance, and precognition.

> Many schools are organized in the following way: grades 1–6, grades 7–9, and grades 10–12.

2. Use the colon to introduce a long formal statement, quotation, or question.

> The book made one irrefutable point: Every good scholar is a good listener.

> Speaking of labor, Abraham Lincoln said: "Labor is prior to, and independent of, capital. Capital is only the fruit of labor, and could never have existed if labor had not first existed!"

> This is the real question: Should the judiciary be given more power than the President and Congress?

3. Use a colon after the formal salutation of a business letter or speech.

> Dear Mr. Tolbert:
> Ladies and Gentlemen:

4. Use a colon between the chapter and verse of a biblical reference.

> Genesis 46:3
> Job 11:20

5. Use a colon between the title and subtitle of a book.

> *College English: The First Year*
> *Poe: A Collection of Critical Essays*

6. Use a colon to separate hours from minutes in time references.

> 12:58 P.M.
> 6:45 A.M.

7. Use a colon to indicate that an initial clause will be further explained by the material that follows the colon. In such constructions the colon could be substituted for the expressions *namely* and *for example*.

> The local government was famous for its inefficiency: the city councilmen were always duplicating the work of the county commissioners.

Be very careful not to confuse this use of a colon with the normal use of a semicolon. Though the two marks of punctuation may resemble each other in appearance, they do not serve the same function.

8. Do not use a colon between a preposition and its object.

> **Incorrect:** He has always thought highly of: Henry James, Fyodor Dostoyevski, and Gustave Flaubert.

9. Do not use a colon after a verb, after the word *that*, or after the expression *such as*.

> **Incorrect:** John has always enjoyed: tennis, golf, basketball, and handball.
> **Correct:** John has always enjoyed tennis, golf, basketball, and handball.

> **Incorrect:** His problems are: awkwardness, nervousness, and shyness.
> **Correct:** His problems are awkwardness, nervousness, and shyness.

> **Incorrect:** Martha enjoys some of America's classics, such as: *The Deerslayer, The Scarlet Letter, The Adventures of Huckleberry Finn, Moby Dick*, and *Light in August*.
> **Correct:** Martha enjoys some of America's classics, such as *The Deerslayer, The Scarlet Letter, The Adventures of Huckleberry Finn, Moby Dick*, and *Light in August*.

Exclamation Points

Exclamation points should be used sparingly. Their correct uses are few and limited. An overuse of exclamation points makes them ineffective.

1.   Use an exclamation point to express emphasis, surprise, or strong emotion.

> The book advised—idiotic though it seems!—that everyone should strive for celibacy.

> What an unbelievably ignorant remark!

> "I'm in pain! I'm in pain! Please help me!"

2.   Use the exclamation point to express a command or to make a fervent plea.

> Pick your toys up this instant!

> Please just let me be!

3.   Use an exclamation point after strong interjections.

> Ouch! That bowl was really hot.

> Man! That was a close call.

Question Marks

Though a question mark is generally considered a terminal mark of punctuation (one that comes at the end of a sentence), it may appear within a sentence. But in any event, be sure not to overuse the question mark. The mark should be used sparingly and in accordance with the rules presented in this section.

1.   Use a question mark after a direct question.

> Did Orville Wright make the first successful flight?

> Robert asked, "Is there any pay increase based on merit?"

Darius—or was it Xerxes?—beat the waves to make them obey his command.

Will I run? is the question every untested soldier asks himself.

But notice that a question mark is not used after an indirect question.

Mary asked what you were going to wear.

2.   Use the question mark with what would ordinarily be declarative or imperative sentences to indicate doubt.

Close the windows?

I have been in the hospital for two days?

3.   Use question marks to indicate a series of queries within the same sentence.

Who will survive? the oiler? the captain? the cook? the correspondent?

Which form of government do you prefer? communism? fascism? capitalism? socialism?

Dashes

Some writers and teachers consider the dash an amateurish mark of punctuation. And though the rules in this section indicate correct uses of the dash, you are advised to use the dash sparingly.

1.   Use a pair of dashes to set off a parenthetical expression that you want to emphasize.

New York, Los Angeles, and Denver—but not Phoenix—are all acceptable convention sites.

If you do get the book finished on time—and I expect you to try—give me a call immediately.

Louis Diat—formerly a famous chef at the Ritz—published a book called the *Basic French Cookbook.*

2.   Use a pair of dashes to indicate an abrupt change in thought or tone.

San Francisco—Mom, I wish you could be here—is a wonderful place.

Words like *sesquipedalian* and *onomatopoeia*—two-dollar words that aren't worth two cents—pervade scholarly writing.

3.   Use a pair of dashes to set off an interpolated question.

Abraham Lincoln—or is it George Washington?—is generally recognized as America's greatest president.

4.   Use a pair of dashes to set off a parenthetical element that contains commas.

Four tragedies—*Hamlet, Macbeth, King Lear,* and *Othello*— are generally considered Shakespeare's best plays.

5.   Use a dash between an introductory series and the main part of the sentence that explains it.

Homer, Virgil, Dante, Shakespeare, Goethe—these were the men who made up his list of the world's greatest poets.

6.   Use a dash to introduce a word or group of words that you want to emphasize.

There is one thing Bob enjoys more than eating—golf.

If we had some ham, we could have some ham and eggs—if we had some eggs.

7.   Sometimes a dash is used to indicate the omission of letters.

Representative G—is not likely to be well received when he returns to the district.

Sometimes Ed can be one genuine son of a b—.

8. Sometimes dashes are used to suggest a stuttering or halting speech.

> I—er—really don't know what to say.

> P—P—Please b—b—bear with m—m—m—me.

9. Sometimes the dash is used in dialogue to indicate an unfinished word or statement.

> Margaret said, "I don't care what you w—"
> "Margaret, now just calm down," her husband warned.

> "Little Jimmy was our whole life and now—" the bereaved mother burst into tears.

Parentheses

The main purpose of parentheses is to set off incidental explanatory information. Commas, dashes, and parentheses can all be used to set off parenthetical information; but the three punctuation marks are used in different ways. Commas are used to set off information that is closely related in thought and structure to the sentence in which the parenthetical information appears. Commas are mild separators; they neither emphasize the parenthetical element nor de-emphasize it. Dashes, however, are used to set off more abrupt parenthetical elements. Dashes are informal marks of punctuation that really emphasize whatever is being set off. Parentheses, on the other hand, are used to set off information that is primarily provided for clarity or for the reader's information. Parentheses are noticeable marks that should not be overused. Parentheses tend to de-emphasize the information that is set off.

> Ralph Waldo Emerson, one of the transcendentalists, is a major figure in American literature.
> > The commas are used here to set off the qualifying element in the least obtrusive manner.

> Ralph Waldo Emerson—an outstanding Lyceum lecturer—is a major figure in American literature.

The dashes are used to emphasize the interpolated information.

Ralph Waldo Emerson (see also his contemporary Henry David Thoreau) is a major figure in American literature. The parentheses are used to de-emphasize the parenthetical information that is inserted merely for the benefit of readers who might be interested.

1.   Use parentheses to enclose incidental explanatory matter.

John Adams (1735–1826) was the second president of the United States.

Sentence fragments (see Chapter 7) are very annoying to readers.

The date of President Kennedy's assassination (November 22, 1963) has been forgotten by many Americans.

2.   Use parentheses to enclose a numerical figure used to clarify a spelled out number that precedes it.

The dental bill was ninety-eight dollars ($98).

The book entitled *Byron's Complete Poetical Works* costs twenty-five (25) dollars.

3.   Use parentheses to enclose a fully spelled out term in order to clarify an abbreviation that precedes it. Do this only the first time the abbreviation is used.

MIA (Missing in Action)

UNRRA (United Nations Relief and Rehabilitation Administration)

4.   Use parentheses to enclose numbers or letters that designate each item in a series.

The camp Bobby wants to go to is (a) too expensive, (b) too far away, and (c) too poorly supervised.

Five of America's most famous golfers are (1) Bobby

Jones, (2) Ben Hogan, (3) Sam Snead, (4) Arnold Palmer, and (5) Jack Nicklaus.

Note: In your writing try to avoid this usage, as it tends to make your papers mere catalog lists.

5.   When the parentheses do not enclose a whole sentence beginning with a capital letter, place the necessary commas and periods after the closing parenthesis.

In *On the Origin of Species* by Charles Darwin (1809–1882), the author discusses the process of natural selection.

Your evidence (most of us consider it invalid) is purely circumstantial.

6.   When the parentheses enclose a whole sentence beginning with a capital letter, place the period or other terminal punctuation mark just before the closing parenthesis.

Are car salesmen really ethical? (For that matter, are any salesmen truly ethical?)

Answer one of the three questions. (Be sure to write neatly and in ink!)

Sandra did not like her physical science teacher. (But then Sandra hasn't liked any science teacher since she failed science in the seventh grade.)

Slashes (Virgules)

1.   Use the slash to indicate alternative expressions.

During the 1960s many colleges offered a pass/fail grading system.

The job requires a knowledge of typing and/or shorthand.

2.   Use the slash to indicate the end of a line of poetry when running two lines of a quoted passage in with the text.

Referring to the battles of Lexington and Concord, Ralph

Waldo Emerson wrote, "Here once the embattled farmers stood / And fired the shot heard round the world."

In "The Deserted Village" Oliver Goldsmith said, "Ill fares the land, to hastening ills a prey, / Where wealth accumulates, and men decay."

Hyphens

Compound Words

1.   Use a hyphen to connect two or more words serving as a single adjective before a noun.

The medic administered mouth-to-mouth resuscitation.

A two-thirds majority will be required to pass the bill.

Henry Price is not a well-known poet.

But notice that the hyphen is generally omitted when the adjective does not precede the noun it modifies.

John Keats's name is well known.

2.   Use a hyphen to form compound nouns of two nouns that show the same functions in one person or thing.

player-coach
secretary-treasurer
AFL-CIO

3.   Use a hyphen with numbers from twenty-one to ninety-nine.

thirty-six
eighty-four

4.   Use a hyphen to express decades in words.

eighteen-twenties
nineteen-sixties

5.   Use a hyphen to indicate a range of numbers.

the years 1832–1837
pages 164–189
Richard Brinsley Sheridan (1751–1816)

6. Use a hyphen to indicate the spelling of a word.

The number is spelled t-w-o and the adverb, t-o-o.

My name is J-o-n, not J-o-h-n.

7. Use a hyphen to prevent confusion in pronunciation when the addition of a prefix results in the doubling of a vowel.

re-elect
anti-imperialist
pre-empt

8. Use a hyphen to join the following prefixes to proper nouns or adjectives.

anti-	anti-German
mid-	mid-America
non-	non-Japanese
pan-	Pan-Hellenic
pro-	pro-Israeli
un-	un-American

9. Use a hyphen to form most, but not all, compound nouns and adjectives from the following prefixes.

all-	all-star
co-	co-worker
cross-	cross-examination
double-	double-breasted
ex-	ex-commissioner
great-	great-grandmother
heavy-	heavy-duty
ill-	ill-conceived
light-	light-hearted
self-	self-concept
single-	single-minded
well-	well-intentioned

Word Division

Use a hyphen to mark the division of a word at the end of a line. The rules for the proper division of words can be complex. In fact, the United States Printing Office publishes a supplement to its *Style Manual* entitled *Word Division*. The volume lists forty-one "wordbreak rules" and has nearly two hundred pages of words separated into syllables. However, most words are divided according to pronunciation. Words occasionally need to be divided to make the right margin look even. It is preferable, however, to avoid dividing a word at the end of a line. When a word must be divided, be sure to put the hyphen at the end of the first line and never at the beginning of the second. Also be sure to consult a dictionary for proper syllabication. The rest of this chapter contains basic word-division rules.

1. Divide words between syllables only.

feu · dal · ism
mul · ti · tu · di · nous
re · in · car · na · tion

2. Do not divide words with fewer than six letters and never divide a monosyllable.

veto
only
breath
cloud
though

3. Do not separate a two-letter syllable from the rest of the word.

in-
-ed
-ly

4. Normally, divide a word between double letters.

reces · sion
com · municate

If a letter is doubled when adding -*ing*, divide between the double letters.

>refer · ring
>expel · ling

But if the word already ends in double letters before -*ing* is added, divide after the double letters.

>call · ing
>shell · ing

5.   Divide words between two vowel sounds that come together.

>residu · ary
>continu · ation

6.   Keep suffixes together.

>relaxa · tion
>persua · sion

7.   Do not separate syllables without vowels from the rest of the word.

>**Wrong:** extreme · ly
>**Wrong:** did · n't

8.   Do not divide the last word on a page.

9.   Do not divide the last word in more than two successive lines.

10.   Do not divide abbreviations (*C.O.D.*, *F.I.C.A.*) or numbers written in figures (*$4,045.55*) or short proper names (*Johnson*).

11.   Do not divide a person's initials or title (*Mr., Dr.*) from a person's surname.

Index